Journeys of the Mind

Stories from the Therapist's Couch

Dr. Marijanet Doonan

Journeys of the Mind

Mind

Stories from the Therapist's Couch

Dr. Marijanet Doonan

Journeys of the Mind
Stories from the Therapist's Couch

by

Dr. Marijanet Doonan

This is a work of non-fiction.
Permission has been granted to use these stories. Names, places, and identifying details have been changed to protect the privacy of the individuals.

ISBN: 978-0-9847094-0-3
Ebook ISBN: 978-0-9847094-1-0

Published by PeterboroPress

Dedication

For

Roy

My North Star

Introduction

Dear Reader,

Come with me and take a look behind the secret door of psychotherapy. Enter a world of revelation and change. A world that, while not easy for the patient or the therapist, can reap much fulfillment for individuals with the courage to persevere. Meet some of the patients who found their way into my office and my life. Their stories open a window into the creative minds of humanity.

People come to therapy in different ways. Some are hospitalized, while others are mandated by the courts. Some are brought by family members concerned about their behavior. Some, unhappy with their lives or jobs or families, seek help on their own, hoping to find a better path forward.

This is not a *how-to* book on therapy. It is a brief look into the lives of some people who function in our world and have sought help. Their stories create pictures of the myriad ways in which people cope.

By writing these stories, I hope to de-mystify psycho-therapy, showing the humor as well as the pathos of people who have encountered obstacles needing change. And, when change isn't possible, show how people creatively adapt to their situations.

I do not apply psychiatric diagnostic labels in these stories, and while medication may have been a component of treatment, it is not discussed here.

Life seeks quiet equilibrium, but the world in which we live often creates disruption. Therapy is a journey in which one can discover oneself. It can be restorative. It takes courage, time, patience, and trust.

I am grateful to my patients for the honesty and trust they have given me in their journeys to find better lives.

Names have been changed to protect their identities, and the patients or their guardians have each given permission to use their stories..

Respectfully,

Dr. Marijanet Doonan

Table of Contents

Chapter 1: Saturday Hermitage   1

Chapter 2: My Way   7

Chapter 3: The Pen and Ink Club   25

Chapter 4: Time is Precious   37

Chapter 5: Go Well, Kira   45

Chapter 6: Awakening   59

Chapter 7: The Year of the Tests   71

Chapter 8: They Come at Night   103

Chapter 9: Uncovering Reality   115

Chapter 10: Cottage by the Sea   127

Chapter 11: Lost Identity   139

Chapter 12: The Tiger Tamer   147

Chapter 13: A World Without Vision   153

Chapter 14: Choices   163

Chapter 15: Therapy and Friendship   173

Acknowledgments   185

About the Author   187

Chapter 1:

Saturday Hermitage

It has been a trying week, one in which the moon was definitely full. I usually choose Sunday as the day to be a hermit, but I have to move it up a day this week. Work has been particularly challenging. So, this week I have chosen Saturday as my Hermitage Day.

Monday brought Mrs. Z and tales of her "wandering" husband, his third "roaming" this year by her account, and this is only June. What will the remaining six months bring to this relationship? I dare not think.

Ah, and then the precocious seven-year-old whose father is in jail for money laundering. The child spent his session regaling me with tales of jail culture: hair shaving 'in all places' to remove lice; toilets without seats; food fixed with no need to use knives.

These are the current fascinations of this inquisitive child. He says he "will become Governor to give my father back the money the current Governor stole from him." Convoluted, yes, but definitely seven-year-old reasoning.

And Tuesday? On Tuesday, I saw the eleven-year-old who brought her pet rooster to meet me. Not many children live in the middle of a major city and have a live rooster for a pet. She let him loose, and we spent much of the session trying to catch the pecking, flapping creature and put him back in the cage. During the chase, she began to tell me of her fear of roosters. That made two of us. I was unquestionably empathetic. Then she told me that she wanted a dog, but her father gave her the rooster instead. She said she hates her father for many reasons, and the rooster is only one. These sessions are sure to be enlightening.

Wednesday night was a long one. There was the teenager our team rescued from the bridge. His girlfriend had asked him if he was gay. He decided life was not worth living. He is safely in the hospital at this point. Hopefully, he will work effectively to deal with his realities and his fears.

Thursday was a full day. First came the sweet lady with blue hair who steals pastries from the corner bakery even though her annual income is over 300 thousand dollars. The court remanded her for this third offense. After several minutes of talking with her, it was clear this was not just her third offense, only the third the courts knew about.

She has stolen an astounding number of different pastries over her lifetime. She then proceeded to replicate them by analyzing the ingredients and selling them under her brand name. No, paying for a confection did not make it a candidate for her investigative cooking. It had to be "borrowed."

She says it is her hobby. She likes the risk, and she will not stop. My sessions with her should be engaging. I wonder what my response will be if she offers to share one of her interpreted confections or decoded recipes.

More? Well, yes. There is Ruth, who is close to retirement age but not there yet. Once, she was a hooker. She hates her parents because they made her go to college to become a teacher. Her teaching career in the local high school has lasted for thirty-six years, but she still feels college was boring and not worth the time or expense. So, she wants to teach girls to be hookers. She feels she has a mandate to do this before she retires. In her mind, she considers it a legitimate trade school curriculum. The local PTA will have a field day if she explains her goal, not to mention the congregation her husband serves as pastor.

Also on Thursday, I saw the sweet, determined patient, Mabel, now in her eighties. Mabel took art classes and now paints lewd nudes. She wants to hang them in the local library. Her bridge club has asked her to resign.

Then, on Friday, I met the patient who thinks he is a chocolate cake. He lives in fear that people are going to cut him up. It is incredible how he folds himself in half as he sits down, carefully placing a white blanket between the bend of his black-covered body. In his world, he is replicating chocolate cake with cream cheese filling. Yes, he is hospitalized.

Late Friday, the administrators told me of a new project. They want me to do what? Train some of the staff for the next two weeks on adaptive devices for paraplegic people who wish to have intimate relationships. Indeed, they jest. Can I stand in front of my colleagues and explain how they could attempt intimacy if paralyzed? And then demonstrate the devices in detail? In some weeks, life is quite challenging.

It has been a demanding and thought-provoking week with unique patients who present compelling situations.

Today is Saturday. I am beginning to think that hermits may have chosen the best life. The phone is ringing, but I do not answer. My mind flies off to dream of camels crossing the desert.

It is Saturday, and I choose not to be at home for anyone, not even for me.

Chapter 2:

My Way

Mabel came into my office, perched herself on the edge of a chair, and clutched her pocketbook close to her chest, conveying the impression that she was ready to leave at any moment.

"I am not here willingly," she announced with a glare. "My children made me come. And, I do not like people—them or you—meddling in my life."

Mabel's children had insisted she see me to determine if she was capable of living independently. They felt it was time for her to give up her car and move into a senior residence. They had been arguing about this for quite a while. Finally, they decided that she should see someone who could be impartial.

Mabel sat rigidly in her seat and stared at me.

"I will tell you what is going on," she said. "I am eighty-five, and I have reached a point in my life when I have alienated most people, including my children. Furthermore, I do not care. I have my friends, my house, my car, my life, and I am fine and happy. My son questions whether I should still drive. He has had three accidents; I have had none. I suggested he not come to visit again until next year. I hope he will oblige."

She took a deep breath and continued.

"My daughter thinks it quite inappropriate for me to play poker until one in the morning. I advised her to get a life and visit again only when she can play poker well."

I smiled as she spoke.

Mabel sat back in her chair and placed her pocketbook flat in her lap. I asked if her children generally came to visit for the holidays.

Mabel replied, "Nope. I convinced them I was going out to dinner with my friends. I would eat tuna fish straight out of the can rather than have them snooping around my kitchen, watching how I cook. They would decide it was time for me to have someone deliver those cardboard 'meals on trolleys' or whatever they are called. Nope, better they stay away."

"I had a physical, and I am healthy," Mable continued. "I have enough income to keep my current lifestyle. I have good friends, and I'm busy. Sure, I like to be alone sometimes, and that is fine. I will never, never, never go to one of those 'God's Waiting Room' places with people who drool and smile and have almost no teeth. They probably talk about nonsense, and everyone eats mush at the same time. There are people there who look at what you do all the time. I will never do that. Even if you think I should, I will not. I will die when I am ready, in my own house, in my way. That is definite, no matter what anyone, including you, says."

As she spoke, I wondered if Mabel believed in God. If so, had she made a bargain with that Being about her plans for the rest of her life? Undoubtedly, if she did, the agreement was signed and sealed on Mabel's terms.

In the next session and those that followed, Mabel described her life.

Gifted with good health, Mabel did not stay away from rare cuts of beef or regular portions of sweets. Wine, which she felt aided her fermented health, was part of every lunch and evening meal. Her car was her lifeline, with the importance that others give to cell phones. She drove everywhere and proudly proclaimed, "No tickets."

Her vacations varied from hiking to exploring new places. She haunted flea markets, hung pictures, tended her garden, tidied her house, and even shoveled snow when needed. She liked movies, especially ones that were a bit "salty." She cooked with gusto and took classes in Indonesian cuisine. Her curiosity was impressive, as were her opinions. She called politicians "crooks," and once had a rather uncomfortable shouting match with the mayor at a council meeting. He just happened to be an ex-suitor. She passed him up for a retired lawyer.

With her lawyer friend, she takes walks in the park and eats out often. They are a much-talked-about couple in her social set, and she is thrilled.

"It is just a platonic relationship," she said. "I tell my friends that, but the salespeople in the lingerie section of Pauley's Department Store think I buy rather risqué underwear for an eighty-five-year-old. 'Dearie, I am not dead yet,' is what I say in response to anyone's 'need to explain' look. I tell my best friend, Winifred, that I am delighted when John stays late after dinner. I know there are peeping eyes behind my neighbors' curtains. It just makes me smile."

Mabel was adamant that she kept her life pretty much together. However, she admitted that she did leave the stove lit one time recently and pots caught on fire.

"I called the fire department, and they came instantly and put out the blaze," she reported. "It was a tiny fire. The firemen were nice about it. The next day, I went down to the fire station with two six-packs of beer and packages of pretzels, the extra salty kind. I bought a fire extinguisher, and they taught me how to use it. See, I know what to do," she said.

Mabel continued. "You know that daughter of mine? She said I should go to cooking school to find out how to turn off the stove. My son tried to find out how bad the blaze was, but he couldn't get an answer from the fire department. Dang, that kid. He overthinks like me."

Mabel took a deep breath and looked at me. She hesitated for a moment and then began.

"And there is another thing," Mabel said. "I also had a flood in the basement. I thought a rat ate the washing machine hose. The repair person came but found no hole in the hose. I didn't remember using the downstairs sink, but the puddle was quite obvious. Maybe I did leave the faucet running," she said. "It was only the basement. The floor is cement. No harm."

Mabel said her daughter frequently called Winifred to see how her mother was doing. Mabel's response?

"Nosey. That daughter of mine has always been nosey. I think she was born that way. She probably checked on the other babies in the hospital nursery when she was born. Watch, she will come for a visit soon to spy on me."

Mabel sat back and took a deep breath.

"Oh, by the way," she said, "I am not out of breath. I am just getting ready to tell you more."

She continued. "The police did follow me home one day. My daughter heard that the police were at my house. She called Winifred to ask why. Winifred told me about the call."

Mabel sat forward and stared at me.

"Darn! You would think that daughter had x-ray vision, knowing what happens clear across the city. Someone must have told her. Wouldn't you think that the police would have more respect for age and arrive in an unmarked car?"

I asked, "Why did the police come?"

Mabel explained. "They followed me home. They were behind me with that dang blue light whirling away with the siren blasting, but I would not stop. You know there are all those 'cop wanna-be's' out there. It could have been one of them chasing me down instead of real cops. They said I was driving too slowly. Why aren't they out looking for criminals? Can you imagine chasing a woman who drives too slowly? What a crock. We pay them for this!"

Mabel sat back. "You can check with the police department if you don't believe me. I think you do, don't you?"

I smiled and nodded my head.

"Good," Mabel said. "I am not batty."

When Mabel's children had first called me and asked if I would see their mother, they had complained that she was filling her house with all sorts of junk. I asked Mabel about this.

"Do I look messy?" she asked. "Are my clothes all rumpled? Are they dirty?" She didn't wait for an answer.

"At different times in my life, I have collected things, many things, and they do not like it. My son and daughter are always complaining about how much 'stuff' I have. I like my stuff, and I do not appreciate all the noise they make about it."

"Know what I did?" she asked. "I fixed those carping children. I collected even more things."

She continued to tell me about her collecting life.

"First, I collected books. When I filled all my shelves, I stacked them on the edge of the stairs between the spindles. Then I went to more garage sales and started to collect cups, not cups and saucers, just cups. Soon, the cups were taking up space all over the kitchen. They even spilled out onto the sideboard in the dining room."

After the cups, Mabel collected hats—caps, beanies, cowboy hats—until she had a room full of hats. She then began collecting old pictures in frames—photographs, prints, landscapes—and finally, just frames.

Mabel grinned as she talked about her things. Her mischievous nature was evident.

"I am happy knowing my children will have to empty my house when I die. I put single dollars under cups and inside hatbands with only a tiny bit of green showing. I taped money to the backs of picture frames. I know my children will be pissed at all the stuff I have in my house. They will want to pitch it all in a dumpster, but they won't. Not once they find a few dollars tucked in with some of the stuff. Those children will be compelled to go through it all to search for the money."

She raised her finger and pointed at me. "And don't you tell them about this. I know this is a private conversation."

As our sessions continued, we spoke about things she could do to ensure she was as safe as possible in her house and her life. She said she would definitely continue to go to her doctor regularly for checkups. She agreed to have Senior Services go through her home with her to be sure there were no tripping hazards or places where she could hurt herself. She had a new, sturdy railing installed on both sides of her back porch stairs. She even had what she called "a senior water cage," a senior bathtub, installed. She agreed to take a senior driver course and made sure she knew how to use the emergency button on her phone.

Mabel felt pretty happy about all that she had agreed to do to keep herself safe. Yet, she said her children would still not be satisfied.

As we continued talking, Mabel explained why she thought her children were angry and wanted her controlled and confined.

"One afternoon, I sat with Winifred over wine and told her I had decided to take painting lessons. I had never painted and I did not consider myself an artist, but lack of experience has never stopped me from trying things. So I signed up for a class in portrait painting. The ad said there would be nude models. I thought that would be fun."

Mabel was animated as she described the class.

"I went early to the first class. I wanted to watch the others. I wondered how experienced they were at painting."

Mabel smiled as she continued.

"The next day, over lunch, I described the class to my friends. The model came in, dressed in a bathrobe. She took her place on the bench and removed her robe slowly. I know I did not pay much money for the class, but this model was pathetic. Her nipples looked like raisins glued onto deflated balloons. I doubt if those flat balloons had ever had a blown-up shape. The model's ribs were sticking out like those I've seen on starving dogs and horses. It sure would be depressing to paint this broad, I thought, so I decided to concentrate on nipples."

"The instructor was not too pleased that I became such a minimalist, but nothing she said swayed me. I just kept painting dried raisins with bones sticking out underneath. I then moved on to prune-shaped nipples. I covered my whole canvas with nipples."

Mabel said her friends were quite shocked but not enough to miss lunch after her next class.

"The next week," Mabel continued, "the model was male. He came into the room with his robe carelessly draped over his shoulder, open to his navel. Then, as he sat on the bench, he dropped the robe from his shoulders. Of course, I noticed the nipples. They were erect, stuck to the wrinkled body. When the teacher asked him to remove the robe, I almost gasped out loud."

Mabel took a deep breath before she continued.

"Oh gosh, that was hard to see. I squinted, but I could not see a penis. Well, not until I got up close and stared. I thought the frigging penis was planted inside the body. I did wonder what the penis had looked like before it decided to be a clam, closed in its clamshell. I was intrigued, and I decided to paint only the penis."

Mabel said she painted several canvases over the next few weeks. At first, she explained, she painted small representations of the male genitalia. "Some were truly wimpy, but at least they could be seen. Soon, I had painted five canvases," she told me proudly.

As our sessions continued, it was evident that painting had become an obsession with Mabel, one she enjoyed. She had turned her porch into a studio and painted for many hours each day and long into the night. Her neighbors came and looked at her work. They were "somewhat speechless," she said.

"Well," Mabel said, "I guess it was rather shocking to see thirteen canvases, each painted with a life-like penis. I told anyone who asked that I had an intimate relationship with each one."

The following week, Mabel announced, "There was a contest, and I entered it. I tried to decide which painting I should submit. Finally, I narrowed my selection to three. I invited my friends over to share my dilemma."

Mabel had one of those pondering looks as she continued.

"It was hard to decide. Should I submit the small canvas with the delicate-looking, shrinking-violet-like penis, slightly hidden from full view? I liked the fineness of my brush strokes on that one. Should I submit the huge canvas that pictured the large penis, definitely an in-your-face, life-like version? Then there was one more, my third choice, the somewhat normal size—well, just slightly enlarged—penis with such careful blending of colors so that it looked life-like and engorged. I asked my friends to help me decide, but not one of them said a word."

"I told them that I thought the largest one would awe any woman. Maybe they would be too awed. And the men, well, they might be overwhelmed. The smallest, delicate painting is lovely. A female judge might be disappointed," she said. "The male judges just might not value the delicacy and beauty over the smallness in size."

In the end, Mabel said she chose the painting of the somewhat enlarged, "just slightly larger than average, almost pulsing penis."

Mabel sat back exhausted after her descriptions. I asked her what happened with the contest.

Three weeks later, she said she received a letter from the contest sponsors. She sat forward and smiled.

"At eighty-five, I thought I had experienced most emotions. I was downright excited to read that I was a winner."

Mabel didn't tell her children about her entry. She only told her closest friends. They all went to the awards ceremony. She said it was great fun, filled with food, drinks, and people milling around, talking about the paintings. Finally, the art director announced the first place winner.

Mabel was visibly excited as she described the highlight of the event.

"Here is what the director said. I memorized it. 'While the subject matter is not usually presented with such boldness, this painting wins the first place award for its richness of color, realistic portrayal, and clarity of the subject.'"

Mable grinned just as she must have when she accepted the first prize certificate.

The following Sunday, Mabel invited her neighbors for brunch to celebrate. She proudly displayed the front page of the newspaper's local section, which pictured her standing next to the winning painting.

"Before my friends left, I pushed the button on my answering machine," Mabel told me. "'MOTHER,' screamed the voice from the machine. 'How could you? Call me immediately!'"

Mabel smiled as she recalled the moment. "I knew that daughter of mine would see the article. She wants me to quit painting, but of course, I will not."

After a pause, Mabel leaned forward and looked at me seriously and said, "I am fine, right?"

In reaction to my broad smile and our resulting conversation, Mabel smiled too. She reached for the satchel she had carried with her into the session. A mischievous grin covered her face as she pulled out a blank canvas. "There will be more to come," she said.

And, indeed, there were more tales of life with Mable.

Chapter 3:

The Pen and Ink Club

The adorable nine-year-old sat sobbing in my office. I thought that no child should have to cry that much. As tears rolled down his face, he said, "I'm the only one in my class not allowed to be in the club. I'm the only one who can't use a pen. I can only use a pencil in school."

His words were hard to discern between his sobs.

"I know I can't make the letters perfectly, but I write the letters the same way with a pencil as I do with a pen."

He moved forward in his chair and continued. "My teacher keeps telling me to erase the letters and redo them. She tells me to keep practicing. She says I can erase them if I use a pencil, but I can't erase them if I use ink."

His body racked with sobs as he kept talking. "Each night I try to make the letters perfect. I do try. I just can't do it. Why can't I do it? All the other kids can do it. I want to be like everyone else in the class. I want to be a member of the Pen and Ink Club. I don't want to be the only one left out."

Michael's mother had told me that he had dysgraphia, trouble with small motor control. Thus, physically writing on a page was difficult. In the age of enlightened schools that encourage understanding of disabilities, this young child happened upon a teacher who championed a "Pen and Ink Club." It was a club to which no one with less than perfect handwriting could belong. Without perfect script, no child could have the privilege of using a pen in that classroom.

Michael kept talking, and his sadness and hurt were evident. He felt isolated, banned from the club his teacher had established with no way for him to become a member.

I asked him if he knew why he had difficulty writing. "My mother took me to the doctor. He tested me and said I had something wrong with my hand muscles. Some 'dys' stuff, but I don't know much about it. Do you? I need to know what it is. I have to get it fixed."

He sat back and looked around the office. He reached for a tissue and wiped his eyes. Then he continued.

"Some of the kids in the class make fun of me. They hold up their pens and giggle when they look at me. They decided that the teams on the playground would be called the 'Pen Team' and the 'Ink Team,' and no one who just used a pencil was allowed on the teams. All the other kids in the class were picked for a team except me. No one wants to be near me. I don't want to go to school ever again," he said, sobbing.

He moved forward and took a pen and a pad from my desk.

"I can write," he said, and he proceeded to write his name. "Not great, but it's okay." He gave me the paper. "Can you read my name?" he asked.

His name was barely legible in cursive writing. The marks on the paper showed that his hand muscles did not allow for an easy flow of letters across the page. I asked him to print his name. Except for letter sizes and spacing, it was somewhat more legible.

"I just can't get my name to work out right when I try cursive," he said.

"Can you print your work in school?" I asked.

"No," he said. "The teacher says everyone has to write perfectly in cursive in pencil before they can try pens."

His eyes again filled with tears as he sat back in the chair with a sense of defeat.

I wanted to know more about this young boy, so we talked about sports and reading. He was articulate and bright. He had traveled throughout the United States to several historic sites, and he described his trips and what he had learned. He knew more about history than most nine-year-olds. We talked about how he knew about so many things and that having dysgraphia did not mean he wasn't smart. He stared, waiting for more information.

I started to explain dysgraphia.

"That's the word," he said. "That's the word about what is wrong with me. Dysgraphia."

He was eager to learn more, and we spent time talking about small motor dysfunction and how that affected his writing. Michael listened carefully.

"So, is it like wires that don't carry electricity where you want it to go?" he questioned.

"Something like that," I said. I promised Michael I would find some pictures of what we were talking about for the next time we met.

"Okay, good. But Doc, how do we fix this?"

I explained that this might not change, but that we would figure out ways to make writing easier.

"Will they help me write my name better?" he asked. "I have to be in the Pen and Ink Club. "No, wait," he said, waving his hands. "Would you tell my teacher these things? My Mom tried to talk with her, and I was there, but my teacher wouldn't listen, and I don't want to talk to her."

The following week I met with his teacher. Her guide-lines were rigid, as was her stance. I explained the problem. She said she understood, but could not make an exception. I told her how it felt for a nine-year-old to be left out. She said sure, she knew that, but all children had to meet standards. We talked about printing and literacy as well as computers. An hour later, she remained inflexible. I told her how I would work with Michael and asked her if we could meet and talk again, and she agreed.

At our next meeting, I brought some materials that showed how learning difficulties occur in children with average and above-average intelligence, some with mechanical prob-lems such as dysgraphia. And, as in Michael's case, it did not have any reference to his ability to learn. She listened, but did not seem convinced that any change in her requirements could take place.

As we spoke, I learned that she played the flute. I asked her if she would try something with me. She agreed.

I drew lines to represent a music staff and asked her to write specific music notes on the treble staff. She did but had trouble getting the notes correctly, especially with eighth notes, sixteenth notes, and rests. We continued for a few minutes with music notation. She had difficulty and put her pen down.

"I've played the flute for many, many years," she said. "I didn't realize how hard it would be to write notes on a staff."

As if a light went on, immediately she recognized what was happening. She said, "I guess if I had to write out the music rather than just reading the notes, it would be much harder."

"We are not all Mozarts," I said, and we smiled.

"Hmm," she said, 'You have taught me something." I could see she was thinking and struggling. "I know the notes. I know the music. But I can't write it well. Yet my brain does function. Right?" She looked straight at me as she asked the question.

I nodded affirmatively.

"Is that what is happening with Michael?" she asked. "He knows the letters, he can recognize them, but for some reason, he can't write them?"

"Yes," I said, "and while you could practice writing the notes and could eventually do it well, that really can't happen with Michael. He has problems with fine motor coordination, which limits his motor skills and affects his ability to write letters. The difficulty extends to other things with writing, picking up things, and even when catching balls at play."

There was a long pause before she spoke.

"I guess I didn't understand Michael's problem. I just thought if he practiced more, he would be able to write well."

We talked for a while about what could help Michael in the classroom. She agreed to work with him. She paused in our conversation and expressed worry about what would happen with Michael and his lack of ability to write well as he got older. She was concerned about his future with an inability to write what he needed to record. We discussed compensation techniques that could work and how Michael could explain his difficulty and ask for help when he needed it.

She sat silently for a long time. Then she said, "I have set certain standards for my students that I feel are important for their development and their future. I have always been sure they were correct, and I am pretty rigid about their importance. But I had never heard of dysgraphia before. I thought Michael was just rushing through things. I felt the prize of being in the Pen and Ink Club would make him work on his penmanship. He tried to tell me. I didn't listen to him or even to his mother. I never even looked dysgraphia up. I am so ashamed."

She looked at me. "How can I explain this to Michael? I will have to change and make exceptions for him. I just didn't realize. I never thought he would not be able to write well because of a physical disability. He looks so normal."

Our conversation continued, and she asked if she could call me when she had questions. With that agreed, we parted amicably. I felt that Michael would find a comfortable space in this classroom and become a Pen and Ink Club member.

The following Monday, Michael came into my office with a big smile.

"Guess what?" he said. "My teacher sat down with my Mom and me and told us she had made a mistake. She didn't know anything about dysgraphia, and after she talked with you, she understood. She told us how sorry she was not to have known about my problem. Isn't that great?"

"Then, guess what my teacher did?" he continued excitedly. "When I got into my class this morning, my teacher asked me if she could tell everyone about my dysgraphia. I said she could, so she told the whole class she had made a mistake. She told them I had dysgraphia, and she didn't know about it. She said I explained to her that it made writing hard for me and that it was just mechanical, like something in a house that didn't work quite right but was okay. She said I was a smart boy but just had trouble with writing. She told them I would be in the Pen and Ink Club and, in front of the whole class, she said that she was 'so very sorry.'"

Michael was beaming.

"I want to do something," he said. "I want to learn more about this dysgraphia so I can tell my classmates more. My teacher said she thought that was a good idea."

Michael and I worked together. He learned how motor skills function by looking at diagrams that helped him understand. He was an eager learner of the intricate details of fine motor coordination.

He began to accept that he was capable and intelligent. He recognized that his fine motor coordination did not impair his learning. He smiled every time we talked about that.

Michael was excited to give a presentation to his classmates. He made cartoon drawings, using a casing around his pencils and pens to grip them better. His illustrations showed the roadblocks his messages had as they traveled from his brain to his hands. He was excited to be able to know about his difficulty and was eager to share this.

Michael invited me to his presentation. His teacher introduced him as an expert on dysgraphia and repeated that he taught her all about it. She told the class again that now Michael was a Pen and Ink Club member.

Michael was quite the "Explainer in Chief" as he told his classmates the details of his difficulties and showed them his drawings. He made sure to say to his classmates that his brain was fine for other things. He was an adorable nine-year-old expert.

When he finished, all his classmates clapped. His teacher asked him if he would give his presentation to other students and their teachers at an assembly.

A wide grin spread across his face as he shook his head affirmatively. He looked back at me with his thumbs up in a victory sign.

Michael was definitely the proudest member of the Pen and Ink Club.

Chapter 4:

Time is Precious

Her silver hair had an errant shock that fell over her face as if it had escaped from her usual perfect coiffure. She stared into the distance as we sat together in my office.

"My life is confused now," she said. "I always felt steady, as if I could handle just about everything. Now I am not sure."

She fingered the edge of her scarf as she spoke.

"This diagnosis was totally unexpected. No one in my family has ever had this. It is just out of the blue. I am not sure what to think. I am not sure what to do. I am so frightened."

Alice had told me about her diagnosis in an earlier session. I had called her because, just as she told me, she had run out of the office.

"I am glad you came back," I said. "We can talk this through, but I know it is difficult."

"Thank you for calling me," Alice said as she leaned forward. "I am doing strange things. I am not myself. I can't keep things together. I do need to talk."

She sat back and stared, then began to speak.

"Did I ever tell you about my grandfather's clock? The clock ticks the minutes. Then the chimes come, every fifteen minutes, with a crescendo of sounds on the hour. I put notes inside the clock on which I have written the dates of important events in my life. It was comforting to do that, almost as if the clock was a friend. Sometimes I think I like the sound of the chimes better than the chatter of most people."

Alice looked at me, and we both smiled. Then she stared at the window as she continued.

"The clock has never stopped. It has never broken. Amazingly, it has kept ticking all these years. I relied on it for a sense of steadiness. I depended on it. It measured my hours and my days in a way that comforted me. Now the ticking is louder. It doesn't comfort me. It is ominous."

Alice stopped and looked away as she began speaking again, sending her words into the air. "My Grandfather gave the clock to me when I was young. He said, 'Tall clocks, long lives.' I thought he knew everything. I am not sure about that now."

Alice looked around the office. "Funny," she said. "You don't have a clock. How do you know when a patient's session is over?"

I thought about the words I would use to answer. This question was not as simple as it seemed to be.

"It's an internal clock," I said.

Alice paused and looked at me. "An internal clock? Without ticking?"

I nodded affirmatively.

"I think I understand," she said. "I am not sure I have an internal clock, but I do have ticking in my head. I wish I could quiet it. The ticking I hear in my head has become extremely loud. It competes with my grandfather's clock. This new ticking invades my days and confuses my life. Together the ticking upsets me and upsets my life. There is no steadying for me from my grandfather's clock now."

Alice stopped talking and again looked around as if she was still looking for a clock. She looked at me and said, "Time! When? I wish I knew. I don't know what will happen next. What will I feel like in a week or a month? What time do I have?"

She sighed. "I always thought it was good to have a clock. Now I don't know." She looked straight at me. "Do you think you can help me? Do you think you can help me live in the time I have left?"

Her tears came, quietly at first and then sobs that penetrated the silence.

"I have to know," she said. "How do I count the time, the days, and minutes? How do I plan my life? For how long? I am not sure my grandfather's clock can help steady me now. Truthfully, the ticking scares me. What will my life be like?

Will I see another spring? Are there any answers? Do you understand? Am I making any sense?"

Alice sat back in her chair and closed her eyes.

"I do understand," I answered, "and you are making sense. The news is disorienting, hard to accept. It is hard to learn how to balance one's life. It is hard to decide how to live in the best way possible."

Alice asked more questions between sobs, but there were no definite answers. Neither of us knew when Alice's diagnosis of Leukemia would end her life.

Over our sessions, we talked about potential treatments that had been proposed to her and their effects. We also talked about accepting the reality of living with a life-threatening disease, putting life into perspective, and understanding that one can choose how to deal with this diagnosis. As our conversation continued, we discussed how to change thinking from things one believes one *has* to do, to things one can *choose* to do.

Alice leaned forward in her chair.

"*That* is interesting thinking," she said. "I need to consider that carefully." She paused and then spoke softly. "I could change my thinking and take the opportunity to *choose* what I want to do instead of what I think I *have* to do."

Again she paused before continuing. "I have been so focused on planning what I have to do, and worrying if I'll get it all done. What will I forget? What should I do? But it may make my life better, whatever time I have left, if I change my viewpoint. Maybe I can try to think about choosing what I *want* to do."

That day, we talked well past the usual time. Finally, she stopped and looked at me.

"Have you lost your internal clock?" she asked. "We have gone way past the session's normal time."

"No," I said quietly. "Time can be an irreverent intruder, an intruder I can choose to ignore."

She smiled. "I like that," she said slowly. "I must think about that. Maybe I can learn to ignore my clock that has no answers."

She stared into the distance and, after a long silence, quietly repeated, "Time can be an irreverent intruder ...."

"I do like that," she said. "I'm going to tell that to my clock, and also to me. It may teach me how to live again."

Chapter 5:

Go Well, Kira

The message on my machine said, "Please, I must talk to you. I want to kill him. Kira."

I knew Kira from several piano competitions I had judged. I called her immediately, and she came to my office the following morning. This is her story.

September

The night loomed long and sleep came fleetingly, as if demons of darkness were determined to rob her of peace. Lying in silence, Kira tried to push her thoughts past them, but they were present in her mind as in her life.

She listened to the music in her head. Her fingers traced the music score on the unresponsive bed sheet, silently "playing" the composition as if on the piano. She mentally critiqued the sounds. Flawless. Yet, in crept her doubts.

That afternoon in her teacher's studio, Kira's hands moved over the keyboard in perfect tempo, aware of Mrs. Svenson at the other piano, marking the same pacing. Kira's hands trembled slightly, but the music resonated lyrically, breathtakingly. In those moments, she felt she was recreating the magnificence the composer intended.

Afterward, Mrs. Svenson, ever reserved, nothing ever quite good enough, cautioned, "You could have played more powerfully while keeping the softness of the piece."

Kira pondered the comment. Perhaps in her determination to make the contrasts, she had played less passionately to create the needed quietude. She appreciated Mrs. Svensons' astuteness, always acting as guardian of the composition.

As her lesson ended, "Go well, Kira" were the words that signaled her teacher's farewell.

It had been a good practice. Yet tonight, the demons still surrounded her.

Could she dare to audition to play solo on the main stage?

Since she was six, Kira had played the piano, practicing each day for hours, but she never had the luxury of unlimited time. She played long hours into each night, the silencer on the piano preventing family and neighbors from being disturbed. Music was her love, but it came with a price. It was one she was willing to pay, but she worried, *Had she paid enough?*

As sleep began to cloud her consciousness, she again heard the music joined by the soft voice of her teacher, "Go well, Kira."

Soon sleep overtook the music, but it was restless.

When the morning light crept into Kira's room, she sat up, silently looking out over New York City below. The clamor of the day floated upward, but Kira heard other music, the music she would play at the audition that afternoon.

As she dressed, she reviewed her last practice in her head and moved to the piano. Silencer on, she played, mindful of her teacher's caution. The adjustment in feeling came quickly, and she felt the touch of her fingers assimilate the soft-ness.

Later that afternoon, approaching the audition hall, she felt a cool breeze brush over her. *Was it an omen?*

She climbed the stairs and touched the unfamiliar door, feeling the cold metal of the doorknob against her hand. Her thoughts were muddled, and her back felt a chill as she again faced doubts of why she dared to be there. Today was the final of this major competition, a chance to play on the main stage of Carnegie Hall if she won. *At sixteen, was she ready?*

The judges were in place, waiting. She reviewed that morning's practice as she walked to the piano. She knew she had played almost flawlessly in practice but almost was not good enough.

Seated, she paused, took a breath, and placed her hands on the keyboard. She began to play and became lost in the beauty of the sounds that blended under her fingers into the lyrical score that had been composed many centuries before.

When she finished, she sat, almost without breathing, and waited.

The committee of judges kept what seemed an endless silence. Kira's mind went limp, trying to reconcile their silence with the flawless performance she felt she had played.

Applause came, softly at first, then loudly, rolling over the audition hall. With a relief that made her feel as if she was wilting, a smile broke over her face. Then, as if in a dream, the words came.

"Miss Williams, you will play on the main stage. Solo!" Tears spilled down her cheeks as she savored the judges' comments that signaled success. And, in the stillness of the hall, she could hear the words of her teacher.

"Go well, Kira."

December

Outside it was the beginning of winter, but the sun warmed the air as if yearning to keep the last vestiges of fall. Inside, a cold chill made Kira shiver as she sat waiting on the plastic chair. Waves of pain shot up her arm as she looked at the ice surrounding her wrist and hand. She moved the ice, but the cold only barely masked the pain.

Kira thought back to the confrontation with her father. It had started as just a conversation. Unfortunately, as had often been the case, a discussion led to a difference of opinion that he rejected. He was angry and, again, as always, out of control. He grabbed her arm and wrenched it with his brute strength, pulling and twisting until he forced her to the floor. Then, as he kept yelling, he slammed the door and left.

Immediately, Kira felt the intense pain in her wrist. She got up awkwardly and hurried out the door, hoping to escape before her father returned. Once safely outside, she looked down and saw the dislocation of her wrist.

Now she was sitting in the emergency room, waiting.

The doctor ordered x-rays, and Kira sat in disbelief in the examining room as the physician confirmed the findings—a broken wrist and broken bones in her hand.

As the doctor continued to examine her, he asked, "How did this happen?"

"It was an argument," Kira replied quietly.

"What kind of argument?" he asked. "This is a serious break. This wrist was pulled and twisted with force."

"I disagreed with him," Kira replied softly.

"Who did this?" the doctor questioned. He sensed her reluctance to answer.

The doctor moved on, explaining how he would set her wrist and hand, leaving it in a cast for at least four months.

Kira felt her body stiffen. "Will I have the full range of motion when it is healed?"

"Possibly," was the response. "The breaks are clean. The hand is out of place, as is the wrist, and we have to twist them back. Most times, one gets full motion with therapy. You have youth on your side."

The doctor called a nurse to help, and within minutes the doctor twisted the broken parts of the wrist and the hand into correct alignment. Only the pale, drained look on Kira's face indicated the intensity of the pain the procedure caused.

The doctor took Kira's other hand gently. "I'm sorry," he said, "Doing it that way is best. The pain is intense, but it is over quickly, and there is no danger from anesthesia."

Kira, stunned by the pain, watched as the doctor began to encase her wrist and hand in plaster.

"What do you do?" the doctor asked.

Kira replied softly, "I'm a student," and, after a long pause, "and a pianist."

"Oh," the doctor replied. "Have you been playing for a long time?"

"Since I was six," she replied.

"Do you play well?" the doctor asked.

"Sort of," Kira answered as the tears began to tumble down her cheeks. She looked at her wrist and hand, now almost enveloped in the cast. The tears continued to come.

"You will not be able to play for a while," the doctor said gently. "Will that be a problem?"

Kira could not reply. Her thoughts were on her music. Her performance on the main stage had been greeted with accolades. The exhilaration was breathtaking and, in the aftermath, invitations to play a dizzying number of concerts had been gratifying. Ahead was the coveted invitation to compete for a space at the Paris Conservatory. A year of nothing but music. A dream. Only one performance remained—the competition the following weekend.

The doctor looked inquiringly at Kira. "Who did this? Has this happened before? Did this happen in your home? Was it a family member?"

The doctor's questions raced through her head, but she could not answer.

As if he knew something she had not acknowledged herself, he asked, "Is it safe for you to go back home? I can have someone intervene to help you."

His words drew Kira back into herself. She looked down as she barely shook her head. "No."

The doctor prodded with more questions, but accepted her unwillingness to speak.

"We will have to send a caseworker to investigate. You cannot have this happen again."

When Kira rose to leave, he touched her gently on the shoulder. She was grateful for his caring. She left slowly, the white plaster covering her injured wrist and hand.

Surrounded by the noise of the city, her emotions vacillated between disbelief and mounting rage. Her pace quickened as she felt anger increase inside, anger that threatened to explode.

She played the incident over in her head. Her whole life in that house came crashing into her consciousness. This had happened too often—cuts, bruises, stitches, twisted limbs, bruised bones—and now this.

She wanted to see her father in court, shamed in front of others, sentenced to prison for his lifetime. She wanted to catch him in his sleep, bludgeon him until he was unrecognizable. She could imagine twisting a cold knife into him as he writhed in pain.

Tears cascaded down her face and she felt like screaming. Instead, she stopped, overwhelmed by her fury. She tried to compose herself, tried to touch reality.

She turned toward the Easy River, always a place of solace for her. The cold of the evening reflected the sudden emptiness of her hopes. Her stomach tightened, her legs numb. She felt drained, empty.

She touched the stiff plaster that wrapped her arm and knew that the events of this day would change her life.

She looked at the river, but now there was no comfort, only silence and blackness. She did not know how long she stared into the darkness, tears streaming down her face. She stood there, sobbing, and wondered how one lives when a dream is dying.

As she turned from the river, the sounds of the city again engulfed her. Overwhelmed, she stepped cautiously into the world again, not knowing what she would do. In the darkness, she heard only one sound clearly, the voice of her teacher.

"Go well, Kira."

And, in her heart, she knew she must find a way.

The Next Day and Beyond

As Kira talked with me in my office, it was evident that her anger, her depression, and her anxiety were significant. She was an amazingly accomplished pianist before this incident, and she had hoped to become a concert pianist.

We spoke regularly to help her accept reality. Over time, she decided that she wanted to continue her studies in music and piano performance. As her wrist and hand healed, we found physical and occupational therapists trained to work with musicians to ensure she had effective therapy.

Kira realized that she might not achieve the success she had before. While her injuries healed, it took months, actually years of practice, to gain a level of performance that was acceptable to her. She began slowly to accept reality. She continued her studies at a major conservatory and gained recognition for her abilities as a pianist.

She does wonder what a year of study in Paris might have been like had she been able to compete. Now facing reality, though, Kira recognizes that she may not have won that spot. She says she is content in her current life, playing piano at concerts, and she often repeats her teacher's words, "Go well, Kira."

She says she is confident that she has now done that.

Chapter 6:

Awakening

A colleague called me, asking if I would see his cousin who had just moved north to live with him. His cousin had had a harrowing experience in his hometown in the South and needed to talk. I agreed to see him, and Curtis came to see me the following week.

When Curtis sat in my office, he said he was unsure what his life was all about. Only a few weeks before, he had left the only place he knew, the small town in the South where he was born. From my conversation with his cousin, I was aware that something had caused him to leave. I asked him to tell me about his life.

"I stayed mostly by myself, trying to make a living and create a life, but it has not been easy," he told me. "I was often lonely and spent some time sitting by a tree down by a creek. I don't know why, but I was always felt drawn to a tree there. It was just something about it. It wasn't that the tree was beautiful or anything."

Curtis interrupted his story from time to time. He described the tree as gnarled and crooked, quite ugly.

He said that "many of the branches were broken, and the few branches that were left rose strangely toward the sky and then hung back down again, looking like huge hands. They seemed as if they could catch people and devour them."

Curtis explained that the oak tree stood partly surrounded by tall pines that shaded it from most light. He noticed that none of the pine trees had planted themselves too close to the oak. He saw it as an omen, and he didn't go too close either.

In talking about the tree, he said it leaned toward the creek as if it had bent to deposit something in the water and could not stand back up again. As he described it, the creek wasn't gentle. It was narrow and edged with scraggly weeds.

The water rushed past the place as if it didn't want to know what was there. Rocks jutted from the shore, and he said he never once thought to step over the edge into the water. It was not at all inviting.

"I always felt that the whole place was really frightening. But somehow, when things were not going well, I found myself down by the tree."

He went there when he was younger and wanted to run away. The place seemed to give him the resolve to go back home again. He used to go there when he got scolded at school. When that happened, he thought he would never go back to the classroom but, most of the time, after sitting by the tree, he went back to school the next day.

Getting older did not change his strange attraction to the tree. He went down by the tree when he lost his job at the railroad and again when his girlfriend, Jenny Mae, left him.

"I guess the darkness of the place fit my mood at those times. I'm not sure I ever got over those things."

Curtis stopped talking for a while and looked at me.

"I hope you know this is hard for me. I am afraid to remember all of it. You see, this one day, I sat further up on the bank. I had never sat that far away from the tree before, but I was tired and didn't want to move closer. It had been a rough day. It had been a terrible month. I lost my job and couldn't find another one. I couldn't even find work as a farmhand, and this was corn-picking season. And, I was overdue on the rent for my trailer."

Then he spoke about a gnawing feeling in his stomach and a worry that spots on his arms might be something serious. He thought that might have been the reason Mr. Ferguson fired him from the grocery store, but of course he didn't know for sure.

Curtis had tried to do things with his life. He had dropped out of high school but had finally gotten a job moving freight. That job lasted several months. Then one day one of the boxes was missing, and he guessed they thought he had taken it. He had not, but they fired him anyway.

He looked at the floor and said sadly, "I thought that Jenny Mae and I were in love, but she left me for Lube Wicker, that strange guy from the next town. I'm not at all over that yet. She said she wanted more friends, and I was too much of a loner. I spent a long time thinking about that. I don't believe I'm a loner. It is just that people didn't want to be with me. "

Curtis talked about Mrs. Krell, the librarian.

"She was mean. I liked to go to the library to look at magazines. I loved the slick ones that had pictures of new cars. I could imagine sitting in one and driving along the ocean's edge. But I was never comfortable at the library. I could feel Mrs. Krell's eyes on me, those beady brown eyes of hers. When I left, I looked back, and she always dusted the table where I sat. Just brushing me away, I guess, brushing away my blackness."

Curtis said he knew that Denny Schmidt, the owner of the town diner, didn't like him either.

"That man seemed to roll back into the wall when I came into his diner. I went there when I had enough money to buy something. I liked sitting on the tall stools and looking through the mirror behind the counter and seeing the people at the tables. Denny Schmidt watched me, too, just like Mrs. Krell. He watched me the whole time I was there. He watched who I looked at, how I sat, and how I walked to the door. I could almost feel Denny sigh with relief when I left the diner."

As Curtis spoke, it was apparent that he thought he was an ordinary sort of fellow. He did not know why he didn't fit in with other people. There was just something that people in these parts did, not anything outright, but things they did that made Curtis think that they would rather he stayed away. He didn't suppose it was anything he had done. He did not know what it was, but it made him feel uncomfortable, as if he re- minded them about something they didn't want to know.

Curtis stopped talking for a few minutes, looked around the room, and then continued.

"The day I have to talk about is a tough one to even think about. I went down by the tree and thought about my dreams for a life with Jenny Mae. I sat further back near the edge of the creek. My future seemed like nothing. No girl, no job, soon maybe no place to live, nothing that seemed like a future. Things hadn't gone well at all. I didn't see how they could ever be right again."

Curtis described that as he sat in the waning light of dust, he thought that maybe, just maybe, there was no reason to go on. He was pretty much alone in this world. His Uncle Carley lived across town, but they did not see each other much.

"My Daddy died from a heart attack, and my Momma didn't talk much after that. All she said before she died was that those men scared my Daddy to death the night they came to the door."

Curtis didn't know who "those men" were, and his Momma didn't tell him when he had asked.

"I heard whispered tales about men from the town who went out at night, but I tried not to listen because it scared me. No one told me anything, and I knew enough that the story would not be a good one if they did tell me."

He continued talking about the time at the creek.

"That day, I tried to think of a reason why I should keep living. What purpose did I have? I could feel my eyes closing as I kept thinking."

He continued his story, describing what had happened. As dusk began to swallow the earth, he looked down toward the old oak.

"I could see the wind blowing the branches. Suddenly I saw something in the tree. It was dark and large. Funny, I had never noticed it before. I froze, and a cold chill ran up my back."

Curtis started to shake as he remembered what happened. He spoke very slowly.

"A crow called out. It circled and swooped down and seemed to peck at the shape on the tree. I was spooked. I wanted to run, but my legs wouldn't move. I wanted not to look, but I was too afraid to close my eyes. The crow circled again above the tree."

Curtis moved forward to the edge of his chair. He reached for my hand and held it tightly as he started to talk again. Clearly, he was afraid.

"Several men stood back as if they were hiding behind the other trees. My body got stiff as I saw that they were men from the town."

"Through the dark, I thought I saw a shape on the tree. The form was human, and it was a body hanging from one of the limbs. I was afraid to keep looking. I saw black hands hanging limply from the form on the tree. I recognized the belt. My body was cold and shaking. I looked up and saw the noose tied around the neck. Then, I saw the face of my Grandfather, hanging."

Curtis was frozen in my office, as he must have been that day. He sat stiffly, squeezing my hand, sobbing.

After a while, he wanted to continue.

"I just sat there, so frightened. A breeze crossed my face, and I shivered. I don't know how long I sat there. I looked around, but no one was there. I finally looked back at the tree. All I saw was a piece of rope tied to a thick branch."

"Suddenly, I knew. I knew why no one talked about my Grandpa. I knew why my Mama had never talked about the men, and the night my Daddy had the heart attack. I knew why people wanted me to go away. I reminded them of what had happened. I reminded them of what had happened in the Deep South not too many years ago."

Curtis sat silently for a while in my office. He then told me that he was so afraid that night, he ran across town to this uncle's house. He said his uncle knew he was upset but didn't ask questions. His uncle made him tea and soup and kept his arm around him as they sat on the couch through the night.

The next morning his uncle asked him what was wrong. Curtis told him the creek spooked him. His uncle knew and didn't ask more questions, just held him close.

Over the following days, his uncle told Curtis that he wanted him to move, to go north and stay with his cousin in New York City to have a better chance at life.

Curtis agreed. He said, "I was so frightened, I couldn't stay in that town."

He made the journey to New York, and his cousin brought him to my office.

As we continued talking over time, Curtis began to realize the truth of what he had experienced. He began to understand why people were reluctant to get to know him. His grandfather had been lynched by people in the town.

Curtis did not understand how this all came about. He began to talk about why the creek held such a pull for him. He did realize his uncle made a decision that could help him, and he was determined to make it work.

As we spoke, Curtis gained confidence. He talked about many things that he hoped to do. He stayed with his cousin for several months, and during that time he worked on his high school equivalency diploma. We found him a job and a studio apartment near his cousin.

It was a beginning, with some success for this young man who took reasonable steps away from what had haunted him in the deep South. The knowledge of his Grandfather's fate followed him in his mind, but his new surroundings gave him a sense of safety and purpose.

At one of our last sessions, he smiled and said, "I feel like I have a new life. I can never forget the South, but I am so glad to be here now. I really do have a new chance to be a real person."

Chapter 7:

The Year of the Tests

Harry's parents brought him to my office, explaining that he needed help—help with school, help at home, help as a person.

Harry was in the second grade and had failed all his subjects for most of the year. His parents had spoken with his teacher, and she told them that Harry would not do anything in class. He would not even talk with her, his teacher.

He had failed in the first and second grades and was held over, repeating the second grade. His parents said he often had wild outbursts at home about nothing of importance and was really quite disobedient. His older brother did not want to be near him due to his behavior.

Harry had seen counselors at school, but would not talk with any of them. He was taken to a private therapist, and he refused to speak with him. His parents hoped he would speak with me.

Harry sat quietly in a chair with his eyes closed as his parents spoke. I asked him if he would prefer his parents sat outside so that he and I could talk. With his eyes still closed, the boy nodded affirmatively.

Harry continued to sit with his eyes closed, but answered my questions about his name and such. Then, when we got to a question about school, he put his hands over his ears. After sitting that way for a few minutes, he uncovered his ears and opened his eyes.

"School sucks, and I never want to go back again," he blurted.

Before I could respond, he continued. "That's all of it. I won't talk about it."

I responded softly, asking about things unrelated to school. Harry stared at the floor for a while with his hand over his mouth to show he would not talk, then got up and looked around the office. He picked up a toy, sat at a table in the corner, and began to play with the toy.

After a while, he said, "You have nice stuff here."

I tried to get him to talk about the toy he had selected, but silence reigned, and it remained until I told him our session was just about over. He got up and put the toy back on the shelf.

I moved to the door and, as he came closer, I told him I would bring Duffy the next time he came, and maybe he would talk with her. He just looked at me, didn't ask who Duffy was, and left.

When Harry arrived the following week, I had Duffy, my therapy dog, with me. Duffy was a Bearded Collie and loved people.

As Harry walked into the office, Duffy stayed by my side. I asked Harry to come closer so I could introduce him to Duffy. He walked over and stood next to the dog. I asked him to tell Duffy to sit and that she would put out her paw if he said, "Shake." He did, and he smiled as he held Duffy's paw.

Harry said nothing, but walked to the shelf, took out the toy from the previous week, and sat at the table. Duffy went over and sat by him, her head near his lap. Harry kept busy with the toy but, at one point, patted Duffy's head.

I signaled to Duffy to come, and she came and sat next to me. Harry looked and asked, "Why did she move?"

I answered that I had called her. Harry stared at me and then said, "Can I get Duffy to come back and sit by me?"

I suggested he sit in the other chair near me and let Duffy sit next to him.

He seemed to think about it for a bit and then got up and moved to the chair I had indicated. "How do I get her to come here, next to me? Harry asked.

"Just hold out your hand, snap your fingers, and call her name," I told him. "She will come."

Harry did, and Duffy moved next to him. "That's neat," he said. "Does Duffy do other things?"

"Yes," I answered, "but she likes people to talk to her."

"Oh," Harry said. "Is this a trick? I don't talk." After a silence, he asked, "Does she talk back?"

I laughed and assured him that the dog did not talk like people, but she sometimes barked.

"I don't like to talk," Harry said. "People think I'm dumb."

"Well, Duffy won't think you are dumb," I said, "and I won't think you are dumb, either."

Harry looked at me and looked back at Duffy. "If I talk, will she play ball with me?"

I assured him that the dog would play fetch if he talked.

"I don't have much to say," he said. "I'm dumb. I got left back this year, and I am with little kids in school now. I don't do anything in school, so they will leave me back again this year. Soon I will be back in Kindergarten, and I will be very tall, and the other kids will be very small."

I decided with this much verbiage from this youngster who rarely talked, I should let him play fetch with Duffy, so that is what we did. As he played, I asked several questions about his home, school, friends, and what he liked to do. His answers were short but showed a good sense of humor as well as sadness, and an awareness that he did not fit in well at home, school, or with friends.

Harry asked if Duffy had gone to school. I answered that she did when she was very young, and I taught her to do some things, also. He kept playing and asked what she learned in school.

I told him he could find out if he asked Duffy to do things by using simple words, and Harry did, using typical dog commands that I told him. Harry enjoyed having the dog respond.

"I like her. She's smart," he said.

"Well, you are doing a good job asking her to do things," I replied.

Harry sat back down in the chair. Duffy sat next to him, and he kept petting her. He asked some questions about Duffy, such as was she a good dog, did she eat her food and treats, did she obey, and we spent some time talking about daily dog activities.

"I don't have a dog," he said. "I might like one, but I'm bad and dumb, so I won't get one."

Sensing an opening, I asked him what he meant about not being good, and he stared at me.

"I'll only tell Duffy," he said.

"Hmm," I replied. "How about telling Duffy so I can hear, too?"

"Maybe," he said after a long pause.

After petting Duffy for a while and trying a few commands that she obeyed, Harry leaned down and whispered to the dog, "I like your name. You are a good dog. You do what you are told. I don't do that."

Duffy put her head on his lap, and Harry smiled.

Harry continued whispering to Duffy about his home and his brother and his parents. He told Duffy that he liked it when his Mother read stories to him and when his parents took him places to see new things. He kept whispering to the dog, just loud enough so that I could hear the conversation.

Harry looked at me and asked, "Do dogs have bigger brains than people?"

His question generated a discussion of smart dogs and not-so-smart dogs. Harry asked if all dogs learned commands, were obedient, and kept learning new things. He bent down and whispered to Duffy.

"I can't learn new things. I can learn things at home and on vacation, but I never learned anything in school."

That discussion continued, and Harry kept talking to Duffy.

"When we go on vacation, my parents make it like school. They ask me to read the signs like my brother does, but I won't do that."

Harry looked up at me. I asked him why, and he just said, "Because."

In several sessions with Duffy, Harry related his trouble with school to the dog in whispers. After a while, he started talking to me.

According to Harry, everything fell apart when he went to first grade. The plain, simple truth was that Harry felt that school just didn't work for him. That is what he had definitely decided.

Harry talked about the stories his Mother and Father read to him. He loved hearing about people who were inventors. He told me about some inventions that he could make himself. Harry knew about snakes and fish and space travel and wanted to know how space suits worked. He helped his dad with electrical things. Harry liked learning. Then he went to school. He said he used to be smart, but wasn't smart anymore.

"Maybe I lost the smart part of my brain somewhere between my house and school," Harry told me. "Maybe the smart part of my brain only works at home. It didn't get to school with me. Something is funny about it, but I know school doesn't work for me! I try to forget that school is there, but it is hard to do when I have to go every day."

"You know," he said, "school is like waking up in the middle of a nightmare and having to dream it again from the beginning."

Harry was concerned that everyone thought he was dumb.

"In school, everyone knows I am dumb because I am in the second grade again. My first grade teacher used to ask me to do things I couldn't do, so I just sat in school and looked out the window. When I did something wrong, the other kids laughed at me, and none of them would talk to me."

He kept whispering to Duffy. "When I was put in second grade again, my teacher asked questions, and I was afraid the other kids would laugh at me again. The other kids asked me why I was in their class and not in my own class. They knew I was dumb, so I just decided that I would never, ever talk in school again."

At one point, Harry started crying. Duffy put her head on his lap, and he hugged her.

"My parents are nice," he said, "but they keep wanting me to do things in school, and I just get angry about that. They don't know what it is like in school. I hate it."

I tried to get Harry to tell me good parts of school and parts that were not so good, but he insisted that it was all awful. He was sensitive and had been embarrassed in school. Now he was afraid to do anything that would cement his reputation as dumb. He would rather be unruly and uncooperative.

I asked him about the first grade and what the teacher had asked him to do.

He said, "I'm not going to talk about it."

One day when he came to my office, I had a picture book about dog breeds on my desk. Harry looked at it and asked me about it when he sat down. I gave it to him, and he looked at the pictures and asked about the different breeds pictured. I read the description of the first dog, and he looked through the pages. He asked about a dog that looked like Duffy. I asked if he would read it to me.

He took the book, threw it on the floor, and started yelling.

"I don't do school things," he said. "I don't answer questions, I don't write, and I don't think. I don't do anything like that, and I don't read either."

He sat shaking in his chair. "I'm dumb," he said. "I can't do those things. I won't do them, ever."

Our discussions had shown that Harry was an intelligent young boy. He retained information that he heard and could talk about it. He had thoughtful questions, but anything he considered school-related was something he feared. From his actions that day and in previous discussions, I sensed that reading might be at the core of his difficulty.

Slowly and painstakingly, we talked about what kids like to do. Harry did not socialize, and whenever anything close to his behavior or school was approached, he changed the subject. When we talked about friends, he looked at Duffy and said, "Duffy has a nice name. My name is stupid. Harry. Who has a name like that? The other kids call me Hairy. No one wants to play with Hairy."

"I want to be Hal," he said. "That's not bad."

He said he had asked his parents about that, but they said everyone knew him as Harry and that it was a good name.

"See?" he said, "My parents thought that was a stupid idea. They think I'm stupid and bad."

We talked about that for a while and often changed subjects as Harry would find negative responses to most things. Finally, we got back around to school again.

"Okay, okay," he said. "You want to know about school? I'll tell Duffy what happened yesterday. You can listen."

Harry bent down to whisper to Duffy. "I knew it was going to be a bad day. I could just feel it. I sat there, staring at the board. Things were written on the board, but I just stared. Mrs. Johnson, my teacher, picked up the green book, the reading book. She smiled, and everyone took out their green books.

I thought about going to the bathroom. That was a good escape, but I use that too often. I just sat and took out my green book."

"Then Mrs. Johnson asked Louise to read. I knew I sat only two seats away, and Mrs. Johnson would call on me. My hands got sweaty, and sweat started to drip down my face. Mrs. Johnson thanked Louise. Then she asked me to read and I panicked. Mike was next in line, and she skipped him. She knows I don't read or talk. She called on me anyway. The other kids just laughed."

Harry started to cry and reached out to hug Duffy, who was sitting on the floor next to his chair. Duffy moved and put her head on Harry's lap. Harry began to talk through his tears.

"Sometimes Jenny Sue, with the red curly hair, laughs at me. She doesn't laugh out loud, but I can see her smirk. She taps Devin, and they smile at each other and point at me. I feel knots in my stomach every time we take out the green book. I know they will laugh at me when the teacher asks me to read."

Harry held Duffy tightly. "I need a dog," he said. "I can take care of a dog. I can teach the dog tricks. I won't be dumb with a dog."

We switched the topic to dogs. "Some just don't obey," I said, "and they need a good deal of training to help them." We talked about breeds of dogs and dog traits, shy dogs, and dogs who might be afraid. Harry seemed most interested.

"Does that happen with people?" he asked. "Do they need more training?"

I nodded. "Sometimes there are things that are hard for people to do, especially in school. Things can be done to help them." I ventured further. "Harry, you have learned many things and I know you're not dumb, but you do not want to learn in school. I think I know why."

At first the boy stared. Then he looked at the floor. "I can't do the things in school. You can't know why. I'm leaving," he said.

He got up and said goodbye to Duffy, and shyly waved to me. Outside in the waiting room, his Mother asked him if he had talked to me.

He looked at me and said, "I talk to her dog, Duffy. Sometimes I talk to Doc, but mostly to Duffy."

He turned and said, "See you next week."

The next week, I had audiotaped the book on dog breeds, hoping I could convince him to listen and maybe even read along with the descriptions. I had the book on my desk when he came into the office.

He sat in his chair and looked at Duffy. "I don't like that book, and I'm not going to look at it," he said.

I told him I had recorded what it said and that maybe he might like to listen and learn about the different kinds of dogs. He seemed interested and asked if Duffy could sit next to him. We took the book and turned on the tape, and I began to turn the pages.

Harry listened and looked at the pictures and asked some questions as we went along. He had more questions when the book was finished. He looked at me and said, "I don't like books, but that one is okay."

He continued, telling me about some of the things he remembered from the book. I opened the book again to the page with one of the dogs he seemed to enjoy. I asked him to tell me what he remembered about that dog. He told me some things, and I asked him to look at the page and tell me more.

"NO!" he yelled.

"Harry," I said softly, "I think some of your problems with school are about reading. You are having trouble with that, and it upsets you and makes you angry."

He stared at me and said, "How do you know that? I didn't tell you."

I asked him to tell me what he saw on the page in the book.

Harry stared. He looked at me and yelled, "How do you know? See, you know why I'm dumb. That makes me AN-GRY!"

He got up and stomped around the office. Duffy walked next to Harry, and this young, upset boy sat down on the floor and put his arms around the dog.

"Duffy, I'm a mess," he whispered to the dog. "Doc knows I'm dumb."

I stood up and sat down next to Harry. "I do not think you are dumb. Talk with me."

"Oh, Doc," he said as he began to cry. "The black marks on the page move up and down. I don't know what they say. They are squiggles, and they move, and I can't figure them out. I'm dumb, and I don't know how everyone else knows what the squiggles say. Even Edgar, who forgets how to get from the classroom to the cafeteria, even Edgar can tell what the squiggles say." Harry held on to Duffy tightly.

I started slowly talking about people who have difficulty reading, but who are smart.

Harry sobbed and just stared at me. Then he said, "My teacher, Mrs. Johnson, wants me to see Mrs. Collins. She said she talked with my Mother, and they both think something is happening with school and me. She said we have to find out what it is, and then she said she I have to talk to Mrs. Collins."

"Doc," he said, "you have to help me. I don't want to talk to Mrs. Collins! She is in charge of SPED. The sign on her door says 'Special Education Department,' and she is it."

I asked him why he did not want to see Mrs. Collins.

"The kids are not supposed to call it 'SPED,' but they do. All the kids who have problems are in SPED. Well, all the kids they find, and they are not going to find me."

Harry sat, resolute about his decision, and stared at me.

"Do you know about SPED?" he asked. Before I could answer, he said, "All the kids talk about the SPED kids. Some SPED kids may be okay, but they don't play on the playground, and they eat in a special place in the cafeteria, and they take that little school bus. I won't go to see Mrs. Collins, not at all, not now, not ever."

With tears running down his face, he pleaded, "Please, help me, Doc. Don't let them make me go to see Mrs. Collins.

I'm okay. Really. I just don't want to go to school. I don't want to do anything in school. I'll just run away."

He took a deep breath. "Doc, reading is like one of those mazes, the huge ones. The mazes that you have to work really, really hard to find the exit. I hate it. I really, really hate it."

Harry was exhausted from talking. I gave him a drink, and he wiped his eyes. "I'll talk now," he said.

We spoke for a while about reading, and Harry told me that he had tried to figure out what the squiggles said, and by the time he sort of figured them out, he forgot what the story was about. Sometimes, he even forgot what the sentence said.

He dried his eyes and told me that it wasn't as if people didn't know he couldn't do anything in school. Everyone knew it. That was what he really hated. He said that everyone just looked at him in class.

Then he started crying again. "It is so hard in school. I have to think of things all the time to get out of reading. I use good excuses, but I am running out of them. The bathroom is one escape. That works sometimes. I can't forget my book, because they always have an extra one. Feeling sick works once in a while, but I can't use it too often because people are beginning to think I have some terrible disease. Sometimes I say I forgot my glasses, but that works only once in a while. Sometimes I drop a pencil. Sometimes I say my eyes hurt, but everyone knows. They all know I'm making excuses because I am dumb."

Harry put both arms around Duffy. He was shaking. He kept crying as he said to me, "My teacher, Mrs. Johnson, looked at me for a long time yesterday. She was waiting for me to answer about seeing Mrs. Collins. I looked at her and shook my head, 'No!' Mrs. Johnson said she would have to see what they could do about it. I know she will want me to see Mrs. Collins. I am too afraid to do that."

I asked him why he didn't want to see Mrs. Collins, and he stared at me and said, "She will make me one of those kids, the ones who have to take the special bus, who are in a special class, the ones who are the SPED kids."

After a pause, in which he tried to speak several times, he reached for a tissue and said, "She'll prove I'm dumb."

We spoke for a long time about special education, about children who were there, and how extra help was needed for them to learn. Harry understood some of it and talked about children who went to Special Education classes, but he was definite. He did not want to see Mrs. Collins.

He looked at me and said, "You know, last night I thought about a brain transplant. Do they do that?" He continued quickly, "That would be the best choice. People would feel sorry for me. 'Oh, my! Poor Harry! Brain Surgery!' I would be in the hospital. I would have my head all bandaged. I would get gifts. That would be better than anyone seeing me going to Mrs. Collins' office. But I haven't heard of any brain transplants, so I guess that's out."

"Doc," he said, "I'm stuck. How do I get out of seeing Mrs. Collins?"

We talked about what Mrs. Collins would do. I told him she would give him some tests to find out what was going wrong with school and reading so she could find ways to help.

He cried and said, "That will prove I'm dumb. All the kids will know because I'll be a SPED kid."

I looked at this young boy, caught with an obvious disability in reading, having the most challenging time in school, trying to fit in with the other children when reading, and everything about school had become so difficult and frightening for him.

I explained testing to him, and that it was a way we could find out what was happening. I asked if he would be willing to have someone outside the school test him. My objective was to have intelligence testing done, which I honestly felt would show that he had average to above-average intelligence. I felt that with that knowledge, the testing in school might be less threatening to him.

At first, his face lit up, but then he said, "But they would have to know about it in school, right? And then I would be a SPED kid anyway."

We talked for a long time about the testing I was suggesting and what I honestly thought it would show—that he was a smart young boy. After much discussion with Harry and his family, he finally agreed, as did his parents.

The testing was completed and showed that he definitely had above-average intelligence with subtests that showed areas of difficulty that affected his reading. The tester explained the test results to him and his family, and he came in to see me, asking for more information about what it meant.

Harry was relieved to hear that he was smart, but he really wasn't sure.

"Doc," he asked, "how can someone be smart if they can't read?"

He struggled to understand some of the things that affected his reading and made it difficult for him. We talked about them and I worked to be sure he understood. We spent much time talking about how there are many ways people can learn things. Harry was interested in talking about that.

I then mentioned that some more testing and some work with Mrs. Collins in school could help him. He was still nervous about the whole idea of SPED and being identified. Finally, he realized his peers already identified him.

I asked him if I could talk with his teacher.

"I'm scared," he replied. "The testing I had was out of school, but it's in school that I have problems."

Eventually he agreed that I could talk with his teacher about his reading challenges as well as his concerns about testing with Mrs. Collins.

My talk with Harry's teacher was productive, and she said that she would make sure that his testing would not take place in the Special Education Center. We discussed that dyslexia was most likely the problem, and knowing more of the specific areas that gave him difficulty could be identified through testing. With that knowledge, they could develop strategies for him for learning and for reading. Mrs. Johnson said that if Harry felt more comfortable, I could come with him to meet Mrs. Collins and sit in on the first test.

Harry was willing to meet Mrs. Collins if I went with him, and so I did. As we walked through the school corridor, Harry kept looking around to be sure no one saw him going to meet with the Special Education teacher. He let out a sigh of relief when we turned toward the art room, which was empty.

Mrs. Collins was friendly. "I talked with your teacher, Harry," she said. "We agree that you need to take some tests that will help us understand what is not working for you. Then we can figure out how we can help."

She spoke slowly and told Harry about the first two tests. She showed him what they looked like. It was obvious he was nervous, but he paid attention.

"Will I try one now?" he asked.

Mrs. Collins agreed.

Harry paid careful attention to her directions as he stared at the booklet in front of him. He picked up a pencil from the table and held it tightly in his hand, which was shaking.

"Harry, you just have to listen and answer the questions I ask," Mrs. Collins told him. "You don't have to read anything or do any writing for this one."

Harry's body relaxed after he answered the first question correctly. In fact, he answered almost all of the questions correctly. Mrs. Collins smiled and told him he had done a super job. She told him that he was a good thinker and knew many things. She then told him about the next test, which had some reading. Harry said he didn't want to read. She coaxed him a little, read some of it to him, and he tried to read, with difficulty.

Harry was relieved when these two tests were over, but willingly went for additional ones in the next weeks. When those were finished, Harry told me he thought there was no part of his brain that hadn't been tested. He was not as scared as he was in the beginning, but he sure was curious.

"What will they find out?" he asked. "Maybe they could map my brain so the squiggles will go down the road to the right place and turn into words I can read. I hope it's that easy."

Finally, it was time for "The Meeting," when Harry and his parents would talk with Mrs. Johnson and Mrs. Collins.

"I'm so scared," he said. "What will they tell me? Can seeing squiggles be fixed? I'm not sure, but I hope it can."

After the meeting, Harry told me he didn't understand all of what people said there.

"Mrs. Collins kept asking me if I understood, but I was afraid to say I didn't. I didn't want them to think the squiggles had spread to my ears. Then there might be more tests!"

He said his Mom and Dad asked many questions.

"Doc, there were papers all over the table. I kept looking to see if I could spy a map of my brain, but I didn't see one. I daydreamed about the map and the squiggles following the right roads when I heard Mrs. Collins say my name. I sat up, afraid of what she would say."

Harry leaned forward in his chair in my office as he continued telling me about the meeting.

"Mrs. Collins told me they knew I was a smart boy. The tests prove it."

He bent down to hug Duffy and said, "At least I'm not dumb." He took a deep breath, "I was afraid that after all those tests, they would know that it wasn't a problem I had with reading but that I was just plain dumb."

He said, "Mrs. Collins said something like the wiring in my brain is a bit mixed up, and that is why I am having trouble with reading and school. I was worried that I would need an electrician to work on my brain. I thought I might need brain surgery. I worried that they would have to rewire me."

"Mrs. Collins told me I have dyslexia, trouble reading, and many people have this problem," he continued. "She showed me how a small p and a small q look almost the same.

I had a hard time seeing the difference. She said there were other letters that give people with dyslexia problems, and there are other things that make reading hard, like letters that move.

Harry said, "Then I froze. They said I was smart, but I was different. I wondered if it could be fixed? Mrs. Johnson read my mind."

"She said it isn't something they can fix, and it is not something that will go away. I'll always have trouble reading, but they can find ways to help me. I will have to work hard, but they can help me in my regular classroom."

"Doc, they talked about some of the other ways to learn things, just like you and I did."

Harry bent down to talk to Duffy. "At least I'm not dumb. I won't have to go to the SPED room. I can learn in my regular classroom."

He kept repeating to Duffy, "I'm smart, and I know it, and other people know it, too!"

Harry took a deep breath and relaxed just a little. He hugged Duffy, then got up and gave me a hug.

"Thanks, Doc," he said. "Duffy is a neat dog, and you're really neat, too."

For once, Harry began to believe that school, even with squiggles, just might be okay.

Chapter 8:

They Come at Night

"It's twilight, and they're coming."

"They come at night—not every night, but some nights. I know they are coming because of the air. It makes me feel stiff. I don't know how they get in. They are there, in that room, in the attic. I have to go there then. I don't want to, but I have to."

Janice, a seventeen year old, sat slumped in the large chair in my office, struggling with her words. She was gaunt, with dark circles engulfing her eyes from lack of sleep. She hadn't talked much to anyone in months, but she needed to speak now. What she said could determine her future.

I encouraged her gently to continue, and she began hesitantly.

"Sometimes there are two of them, sometimes three. I can't see the creatures' faces—they cover them—but I can see their shapes. I hear them when they talk. They don't walk. I mean, it's like they walk, but nothing touches the ground. They wear grey, all grey. They go to the side of the room, near the window, and look at me. They tell me what to do, and I know something frightening will happen if I don't do what they say. Sometimes they just talk in a low wail-like voice. Other times they yell."

Janice sat shivering in the chair. Her eyes darted back and forth across the room.

"I have to do what they say. The creatures put strings on my shoulders, and when they want me to do something, they pull the strings. Sometimes they just sit and stare at the window. Sometimes they almost drag me to the window to open it, even when it is freezing. I have to open it. I don't like the window. No one ever comes to the window. It's on the third floor, but I'm afraid someone will come through the window and get me. I just feel it. The visitors frighten me. I don't like them."

Janice's words were muffled, her mouth covered by a wool scarf pulled close around her face despite the warm summer temperatures outside. As she spoke, she unraveled the wool from the scarf, leaving a puddle of loose strands in a heap on the floor next to the chair.

She sat forward, glancing at the windows in my office as if she expected these "visitors" to come in through them. She sank back into the chair and wrapped the scarf tighter around her face. Eventually, she resumed talking.

"Once, they told me to read a book. I had not heard of it, but I found it on my bed. It was about a girl who turned into a statue. It made me feel frozen, and some of the print on the pages felt cold. Sometimes the visitors are only there for a few hours, but other times they stay the whole night. I am tired from their visits. I want them to go away. I don't know how to make that happen."

Her muffled voice continued. "On Sunday, they told me to have a drink early in the morning. When I went to the kitchen, a full glass was on the counter. I drank it, as they said. It was warm and slipped down my throat. I had to drink it, but I don't know what was in it."

At times, it was difficult to determine what was real in what Janice said. Her house did have a room on the third floor in the attic, and it did have creaky floorboards that made noise, and her parent reported that she did go up there at night. She did have a bedtime drink each night and a drink each morning set out for her by her mother, but she also talked to people who were not there. Their visits were real to her, though. They were as authentic to her as a visit with a neighbor, except she did not feel equal to them. She thought they had control over her. Her actions showed that, in her mind, they did.

She stared at the ceiling, continued to unravel the scarf, and took deep breaths. I asked her if she wanted to stop talking now, and we could continue later. She started shaking and looked around the room. She sank back into the chair and pulled the scarf tightly around her.

"No," she said. "I think it is safe here. Please stay with me."

She rocked back and forth, and then, slowly, started talking again. "They told me things I could not do. They told me I could not go out. They said I had to dress all in grey, no colors. I had to get rid of my other clothes."

I asked her what she did with her other clothes, even though I knew the story from her parents' intake report. I wanted her to tell me.

"I made a fire on the back porch and burned all my clothing, but I saved anything that was grey. The fire got big, and the fire department came. They put the fire out, and then they tried to talk to me. I screamed and ran into the kitchen because I was afraid. The firemen followed me."

Janice closed her eyes and started to shake again as she continued.

"There was a knife with a shiny blade on the counter. I took it and stabbed one of the firemen. I saw the blood pouring out of his hand, and he screamed and tried to grab me. I ran to the attic."

She stayed shaking in her chair. I waited until she was able to speak again.

"My father came to the attic but not with a fireman, with a policeman. My father said they would take me to the hospital. I screamed. I remembered that my mother and father had talked about taking me to the doctor's before this, but I ran to my room and locked myself in then. Now they said they would take me to the hospital because this policeman said I had to go to the hospital or they would have to take me to the police station. I started screaming because the creatures told me I could not go out of the house. The policeman and my father just picked me up and took me here."

Janice stopped and closed her eyes. She sat back and said she wanted to stay right there until she could think again.

According to her parents' intake report, the recounting of how Janice got to the hospital was accurate. The questions, that needed to be asked now, which may not have an answer, were what triggered her behavior, her belief that creatures came to visit her at night in her attic, and that these creatures controlled her.

Janice was exhausted from telling her story. She returned to her room in the hospital and slept for hours. Over the next few days, she said little and slept much. Medication helped her to slowly adjust to a routine of sleeping, eating, and finally, being willing to move out of her room.

Our conversations continued. In some sessions, Janice said little, but eventually she became more comfortable and spoke more. In one session, she described a class trip to the Indian Point Nuclear Power Plant in Buchanan, New York. She whispered, saying she "wanted to be sure that the creatures did not hear her."

"The workers at the Nuclear Plant wear green clothes," she said. "Every worker wears green. I had bumps on my skin after I went there. The bumps turned to brown spots on my arms and my face. I was radiated."

Janice's face was freckled. I assumed her arms were, too, but her tightly grasped sweater did not allow for confirmation. I asked her if she had spots on her face before she visited Indian Point.

"I don't know," she said. "Maybe, but these spots now are from radiation. I can't go outside because someone will radiate me again."

Asked how she knew that someone had radiated her and that it would happen again if she went out, she looked around and whispered, "The visitors told me. They told me aliens took over the nuclear plant, and they were the ones that radiated me."

It took time to get Jaina to speak more about her visit to Indian Point and when the "creatures" started to visit her. Eventually, she was able to talk about them without whispering, recognizing that they were not in my office. Her fear of radiation was tied to these creatures. Somehow, even though she was afraid of them, she felt that the strange visitors protected her. It was hard for her to think that she did not have to obey them or that she did not need them.

With careful encouragement, she described the creatures to me and, after many sessions, the clarity of what they looked like started to diminish. At a point in our sessions, she agreed to a physical exam and listened as the results indicated no radiation. She did not acknowledge that she accepted the results.

In time, she agreed to walk outside. When this was first suggested to her, she shivered and refused. However, as her ability to describe the creatures diminished, she tentatively agreed to go outside for a few minutes, the first time in months. After a while, she would go out and walk for more extended periods and even enjoy the sunlight.

She asked questions about Indian Point, and the creatures that she felt frightened her and yet protected her. She asked for books about nuclear power plants and about how they safeguarded people from radiation. She wanted to know more about the safety of the water in the Hudson River, the banks on which the Buchanan, New York nuclear reactors were built.

Janice accepted reality slowly. She still refused to wear anything that was not grey. She said the creatures told her that "all colors are bad. They all have radiation, all except green and grey."

She still worried the visitors would come back to her house. A planned day trip to her home created much anguish for her. A counselor accompanied her, but she insisted on going to the attic room herself. Next, there were two overnight visits with a counselor, who stayed in the house with her and her parents.

Medicine helped control Janice's symptoms. Eventually, she was able to go back home and continue regular therapy sessions as an outpatient. Today, she is primarily calm and relaxed. The visitors have not returned, but she still worries about them. She goes out shopping and meets with friends from a small group therapy session.

She still will only wear grey. She smiles and says, "It is my protection."

Chapter 9:

Uncovering Reality

I would like you to meet Rita, one of my patients. Step into her world, as I first met her. Observe with me as we try to understand what she faces every day. There are many children like her in our neighborhoods. They are the children of our acquaintances who need appropriate education in our schools, children with difficulties that need solutions.

I first met Rita in her school. She was an attractive young girl with a posture that showed her reluctance to be noticed. Seated, she seemed as if she was "rolled into herself." Her reading book was tucked into her arms, not held in her hands or placed on the table. Her long blond hair hung below her shoulders, hiding her face, which she kept downward.

The teacher guided the reading of this special group of fourth-graders. The three other students kept up as well as they could, but Rita did not seem to follow along. I felt anxious as her turn to read out loud came closer.

"Rita, would you read for us?" Asked the teacher.

The young girl did not move, but began. "I was...," and then there was hesitancy.

Rita was silent. I could not see if her eyes moved, but she did not speak. The other students did not make a sound. Rita sat and looked at the page.

Finally, the teacher said, "Expecting," supplying the next word in the sentence. "Go on," she said. "What is the next word?"

"Her to...," Rita said, and then another pause.

"It is something people do when they are happy," prompted the teacher.

Rita did not respond.

"Can anyone give us that word?" asked the teacher.

One of the other students said, "Smile."

"Can you read the whole sentence, Rita?" Asked the teacher.

Rita began. "I was ex…ex…ex…her to s…s…smile."

"Good," said the teacher. "When do you smile, Rita?"

A long silence and then the quiet words, "When I go to sleep."

I watched as the reading session continued, noting that Rita did not follow. Her body language told that she did not seem to grasp the story's meaning, and there was no sense of how she felt. When the session ended, Rita closed her book, got up, and reached for her backpack, looking like any ordinary student. However, she was not that at all. She seemed unable to keep pace, even with other special students in that basic reading class.

After the students left, the teacher turned to me and said "They have all done so well. You should see where they came from."

"Rita?" I asked.

"Oh, Rita, she is doing very well. She is just a bit slow and needs special help. I work with her because we don't have a special education teacher yet, but I don't have enough time to do all the other things she needs. She will come along, though," she said.

I stepped back and silently wondered

Later, I read Rita's records. To the school, she was "labeled" Educable Mentally Handicapped. Her full-scale I.Q. was listed as 74, considered to be low borderline. Earlier testing indicated similar results with limited comprehension and poor memory.

Rita was left-back—"held over" is the new euphemism—in the second grade. It was easy to project that she could face the same fate at the end of this current year.

The goals written for her in her federally mandated Individual Education Plan included improving spelling, comprehending complex sentences, as well as other goals that seemed beyond her reach. Nothing was written about the child herself.

Nevertheless, there was more to Rita than that. Her IEP said nothing about her strengths, which would have given clues to ways to educate her. My mind reeled at the thought of what daily life must have been like for her. How much did Rita hurt inside due to being "held over," facing failure daily, and of never matching up to her classmates?

Think for a few moments how much you would hurt if you were required to go to work each day where you could only fail? Would you be aware of how inadequate your work was compared to your coworkers? Would you know if others recognized that your work was inferior? Would you be embarrassed? Would you be depressed? How would you feel if you had to be in this situation for several more years?

Laws required that Rita be educated as much as possible in the same classroom with her peers—peers who were interested in long designer nails and clothes that showed off beginning womanhood. Peers who engaged in chatter and required the ability to sing along with the latest hits and recognize the newest idol. Peers who had energy unbounded and sapped up every piece of Hollywood fame and style. Peers who knew well when someone had been "held over," if someone did not have the latest style, if someone did not reach acceptable levels of participation in school. Peers who could become bullies.

I thought ahead after this observation. I knew that the route ahead would be challenging for Rita. I had to discuss with her parents that there was quite possibly a ceiling on their daughter's ability to succeed in school. This is a painful possibility to accept when, just a few years before, that tiny bundle, held close on her birth day, had the promise of the entire world.

I knew, however, that I had only one part of Rita's story, and my individual sessions with Rita might tell me more about her.

The sessions I had with Rita were learning ones for her and for me. Rita began to talk more and ask more questions. One day she noticed a plaque on my wall written in calligraphy. She picked up colored pencils from my desk and began to copy the letters on some paper. It took her a while to do it, but she did a great job, copying the letters almost precisely. She held up her work and smiled

"I like this," she said "I can do this."

This could be an ending to this story, a possible path to a new approach, but it is not.

I had noticed several times that Rita used words—expressive words—quite correctly, more advanced words than someone with her listed limited intelligence might know.

After she said, "I can do this" about the calligraphy, she added, "Almost perfect. Exquisite." My mind clicked into overdrive as I started to put together my observations about Rita.

She was always impeccably dressed. Her mother said she selected her clothes and dressed herself.

Rita had a watch with a dial that she checked as each of our sessions neared the end. When I asked her the time, she was always accurate.

Rita said she watched tennis on television and, although she had never played the game, her understanding of the rules and scoring was accurate. She knew more than I would have expected about several of the world-known tennis stars.

The picture of this young girl, functioning so poorly academically and seldom speaking to others, did not compute with her interest in tennis, her ability to follow tennis stars and their lives, and the advanced vocabulary she used. These indicated more intelligence than had been reported by her school testing. I needed to go further to understand the dichotomy between what Rita presented and who she really was.

An only child, Rita lived with her mother and father. She said that her best friends lived next door but she did not answer my questions about them.

We spoke for several weeks, and I continued to feel that something had blocked Rita's ability to function and that she was more intelligent than reported. In one session, I approached the subject of physical maturing. She sat back in her chair and gripped the cushion tightly.

"Some girls in school are quite grown up. You don't have to be grown up to have boys want to touch you," she said.

When I asked her to talk more about that, she became silent. I talked around the subject and then, after a while, asked her directly if anyone had touched her.

She looked directly at me and said, "Not now. I stay close to my mother." Then she said, "It's not bad to let people touch you."

It is not necessary to present detail by detail the intense conversations that followed. They uncovered that something sexual had occurred. This had frightened Rita, and she tried to repress it by staying quiet and locking everyone out as much as she could.

Rita eventually told me that two of neighbors, her friends, two boys who were several years older than she was, had played with her in games of doctor and patient. This molestation lasted from when she was six until a year ago.

The young girl cried and said she had to pretend she couldn't do anything in school. She didn't care what people thought as long as they stayed away from her.

Rita was no longer my patient with possibly limited mental ability. She was a patient who was a victim, who hid what had happened and retreated into herself, afraid of the outside world.

Rita did not want her parents to know, but after we talked she realized they must be told. She was totally embarrassed to have them know. The shock of what their daughter had been through affected her parents deeply, as one might imagine, and they want to do something to be sure these young men were punished.

But this posed a significant problem. It would have been Rita's word against those of the young men. Since Rita's school records showed that her tested intelligence was limited, others might doubt her story. She and her parents understood this dilemma, and new testing was completed. Despite her limited fund of basic knowledge due to years of shutting down, she tested in the normal range of intelligence.

Her parents contacted an attorney and, as expected, the police became involved.

The case went to court and Rita, although rattled by the turn of events, was willing to testify in court. She gave her statements and answers questions via closed-circuit video to avoid facing the young men she was accusing.

They were convicted, and both were given legal punishment.

For Rita, it was difficult for her to understand that she was not at fault. She accepted this slowly and started to believe in herself. Private tutoring was arranged to help her reach a point where she could return to school in a grade close to her age. She enrolled in a private school, where she did well, and is scheduled to graduate from high school next year.

It was a long route for Rita, and doubts still cause her to question herself, and her participation in what happened. She eventually accepted that she had done the right thing to expose the boys she then realized took advantage of her. She said she was relieved to have talked about it despite the difficulty involved.

Today, she enjoys learning and is happy to have others know she is capable. Hopefully, as time goes on, she will be even more comfortable in her world.

Note:

In therapy, what is presented initially by the patient must be thoughtfully considered. However, the therapist must go beyond this. Something very different may be occurring. The patient's story is often told not just through words but in subtle actions and expressions to which the therapist must be alert.

The importance of awareness and caution, of observations, of using defined questions, of moving beyond superficial testing data, are vital ingredients. The ability to uncover and understand the whole person is a key to achieving appropriate resolution for the patient.

Chapter 10:

Cottage by the Sea

Life often brings unexpected complexity with events we cannot anticipate. When related to family and possible parenthood, entanglements can create lasting ramifications.

Angie came to my office for help in demystifying a puzzle that had unsettled her life as she looked for a new home. For the first four years of her life, she had vacationed with her parents on Cape Cod, Massachusetts. Her memories of those times were dim, as her parents died when she was six and her aunt and uncle in New York City raised her. As an adult, Angie found herself drawn back to Cape Cod and spent summers there, enjoying the activity as well as the quietude. She loved to drive around the small towns and savor the different scenes each presented, often wondering what it was like when she was there with her parents.

Angie had spied the cottage often as she drove along the sea road. It sat at the top of a cliff overlooking the ocean. It appeared worn and somewhat dilapidated, but something about it intrigued her. It just seemed to beckon to her.

One day she decided to stop. Given the height of the grass and the unkempt bushes, she assumed no one currently lived there. She parked at the edge of the lawn, walked up the path, and peeked in the window. There wasn't much to see: some old rustic furniture, a fireplace with a basket of papers nearby, a compass, and a large map with pins in it. Everything had layers of dust, even more than what covered the windows.

She tried the door, but it was locked. Anxious to see more, she walked through the tangled vines and grasses around to the back of the house. The back door, too, was locked.

It was strange, but she felt as if she knew this house somehow, as if she had been there sometime before.

The sea was magnificent. It came up to the cliffs' edge, the rocky crags below causing the water to lap with perfect rhythm. As the salt air brushed her face, Angie knew that she wanted to own this house at the top of the hill.

She walked back to the car, imagining what it would be like to live there. She decided to find out more about this place.

The following day, a round of inquiries uncovered the name of the owner. Mr. Spenser was an older man who had been a sailor and now lived in Cambridge, Massachusetts. Within a week, she had made an appointment to meet with him.

The next week, she went to Cambridge and was ushered into a bright sitting room by Mr. Spenser himself. Tall and gaunt with gnarled hands and a wind-swept face, he was the living embodiment of the image of everyone's sailor.

"So, you want to buy my cottage by the sea?" His eyes pierced hers as he spoke.

"Yes," Angie replied.

"Haven't been there in over a year," he said. "Great house, amazing spot. Worth a fortune, you know."

She could feel her spirits dim. Maybe Mr. Spenser wouldn't sell and, if he did, perhaps she couldn't afford it. Before she could say anything, his voice interrupted.

"So, what do you like about it?"

"The sense of it," she replied. It was hard for her to explain, but there was something about the place—almost an aura—that made her feel she knew it in some way. It might sound silly, she thought, but it seemed to speak to her. "It sits there at the edge of the cliff, perched over the sea. It is a small house, yet it has a commanding presence in that site."

"Yes, it does that," he said, "and it does it very well. Compelling, wouldn't you say?"

Before she had a chance even to nod, he continued. "Do you sail?"

"Some," she replied.

"What is the largest craft you have handled?"

"A Cal 28."

"Great sailboat," he said. "But only a twenty-eight footer? Why, I have captained boats many times more massive, in storms, in rough seas, even without instruments. Sometimes I thought I wouldn't make it back to shore. It was mighty satisfying after those trips when I saw my house up there on the hill. A special place to me, that house. Someone exceptional has to own it."

He stared at her and then continued, "What would you do there, in my house?"

She thought about his question and said she would live there. "I would write books overlooking the sea. The sound of the ocean would create the background and could be comforting and inspiring."

He asked if she would sail. She answered cautiously in the negative, wondering if he would make that a requirement for ownership.

"Hmm," was the only sound he made as he stared at her. Finally, he replied, "Good. One sailor in a house is enough, and I was much more professional than you. Did I tell you about when I sailed to Aegina, Greece?"

Before she could answer, he was immersed in tales of sailing the Aegean Sea and about his docking adventures at different Greek ports. She realized then that this would not be a short visit. She felt that if she were ever to own this house, she would have to tell him about her life as well as relive the sailing days of Mr. Spenser.

Still, he was most impressive. His face expressed the excitement he had experienced in his sailing days. He smiled and grimaced as his voice's tones varied with the parts of the tale he was telling. He was an engaging man.

Mr. Spenser then asked her what she did to make money, and she replied that she wrote novels about people and adventures.

"Do you make enough money to buy a house like mine?" he asked.

She looked at him cautiously, not knowing exactly how to answer. "What would you ask for the house?"

"Not sure." He puckered his lips. "It is a unique house. My grandfather had it built. When he died, he left it to me."

Silence filled the room. He walked to the window and looked out for several minutes. Then he turned and looked at her.

"The cottage is my past, part of my history. It is comfortable to know it is there." He paused for a long time. "I must go back and see the cottage again before I decide. Let me take some time to think."

Angie left, hopeful that Mr. Spenser would be willing to part with his cottage. Two weeks passed, but she resisted the urge to contact him. Each day brought hope that he would call. She drove by the cottage, thinking he would be there, looking at his house. Finally, after agonizing weeks, the long-awaited phone call came.

He invited her to lunch at a local restaurant. After more questions about her life and more tales of his sailing days, he asked, "Would you like to see the inside of the cottage?"

Her mind raced as she nodded affirmatively.

Mr. Spenser handed her the keys. "Look at the cottage very carefully. Then call me, Angelina. Now I must go. I have a meeting to attend."

After he left, she sat quietly, surprised that Mr. Spenser had called her "Angelina." Everyone called her "Angie." She pondered that, but her mind focused on what she would see inside when she went to the cottage.

Her hand shook as she put the key in the door. The cottage was spotless. Slowly, she walked through the rooms and looked out the windows. Something about this place was extraordinary to her. It seemed as if she knew it in some way.

She stepped into the sunroom overlooking the sea. The view seemed endless. On the table, there was a ship model with a note.

This replica is "The Angelina," the ship of which I was the Captain on a mercy mission to Honduras.

Her eyes widened. The *Angelina?*

Next to the model was a handwritten journal, its pages yellowed with age.

"The Voyage of the Angelina to Honduras"

by Trevor Spenser

At the side of the table was a large folder addressed to her. Angie opened it to find a letter.

Dear Angelina,

I met your father in Honduras when he was head of the Mayan archaeological project at Copan. We became friends. After a while, your mother came to visit and stayed for several months. I fell intensely in love with her, but she was married. Shortly after Christmas, she returned to the States. Your father followed her in the late spring when his work at Copan was complete.

In early August, I received the enclosed.

Trevor Spenser

Angie opened the smaller envelope and discovered two photos inside. The first was a picture of her mother holding a tiny infant. On the back was the inscription:

Our new baby princess, "Angelina."

The second photograph was of her mother and father holding her hand when she was about four years old, standing in front of this very cottage. On the back was the inscription:

Trevor,

We loved vacationing in your cottage.

Thank you.

Angie's body shook as she stared at the old photos. *What did this mean?* She was numb. After a while, she placed the pictures on the table and looked at the other papers in the folder. They were Mr. Spenser's *Will*, dated twenty years ago. A folded paper protruded from the document as a bookmark. Turning to the marked page, Angie read:

Upon my death, my cottage by the sea (noted earlier under My Possessions) is to be given to Angelina S. Cartwright.

Angelina's mind raced and her body stiffened. Her hands shook as she held the paper. So many questions crossed her mind. Her eyes stared at the words on the page. A red star and an arrow in the margin of the page pointed to the bottom.

It was the codicil to the *Will*, dated just the previous day, signed by Trevor Spenser and notarized by his attorney. It read:

> *As of this day, I give my cottage, as noted above, to*
> *Angelina S. Cartwright.*
> *She will be the new, unencumbered owner.*
> *I wish her a long and happy life in her cottage*
> *by the sea.*
>
> *Trevor Spenser*

Confused and conflicted, Angie sat at the table holding the two photos and sobbed. She did not remember the part of her life they reflected, but indeed, this cottage was part of her history.

She wanted to scream at the ocean and ask all the questions running through her head, to run to Mr. Spenser and learn more. She sat trying to figure out what she would do to know more of this puzzle in her life.

After a while, her phone rang. She answered it hesitantly, unsure of so many things at this point.

It was Trevor Spenser.

"Angelina, may I come to the cottage? We can talk."

This story was first published in a slightly different version in Ripples, *an anthology by Island Writers Network, Hilton Head Island, S.C. in November, 2021.*

Chapter 11:

Lost Identity

At 65, Parker said he wanted to die. With a successful career as an investment banker behind him and a loving family around him, he sat in front of me, stared at me, and said, "I am done."

Parker was brought to see me when his wife, Elena, found him in the garage, locked in his car with the engine running. As they sat in front of me in my office, she said through her tears, "Please help us. I want Parker to be with us. He does not want that anymore."

Parker looked at her and then looked at me. "I am not good for anything anymore. I can't even kill myself successfully."

With his wife sobbing and trying to hold his hand, Parker started speaking.

"I've had a good life. I worked my way up to a great salary. My family lives in comfortable circumstances. My son and daughter are both married, but don't want to have children. My wife is attractive, and she will find someone else. I've done it all. There is nothing left for me. I am retired, miserable, and I want out of life."

The starkness of his comments, mixed with the sobs of his wife, created a tense atmosphere in my office. I asked them both if Elena could sit outside so I could speak with Parker alone. They agreed.

Parker began to tell me about himself and his life. Like many people, he thought of living a great retirement life with no more daily responsibilities.

"Retirement sounded like Shangri-La," he said. "I took the golden parachute for retirement and gave up my corner office, secretary, business cards, expense account, and other perks of successful employment. I had a good retirement nest egg, and I wasn't worried. I looked forward to a leisure-filled life. We traveled and visited family. We did pretty much whatever we wanted for a whole year. It was all boring. I had no structure, no purpose. I have no use now as a person."

We talked for a while about his work, and Parker described the somewhat typical corporate experience, with responsibilities and respect for his ability. We talked about leisure activities so that I could get a better picture of who he was.

"I used to like golf," Parker said. "It was an enjoyable game. Now, it seems that everyone I play with, even those people from before, see it as competition. I didn't recognize that before. They have to be perfect, the best. They have to win every round. They are trying to climb the 'ball-in-the-hole' corporate ladder with a game. It is not a game to them. It is not fun. It is cutthroat. It is their very existence."

"Now I have no hobbies, no interests," he continued. "My family is nice, but I never realized that just being with them all the time would be so boring. I can't say that. They would not understand. I love them, but this isn't life. There is nothing to it now."

I told Parker I had some thoughts I wanted to share with him. I elicited a promise that he would come back the next day to talk without any attempts to hurt himself. He agreed, and we told Elena our plan. She told him she would watch him every moment, as I expected her to say.

Parker stared and said, "That I am sure of."

Parker returned the next day, and Elena sat outside waiting for him as we spoke. We discussed returning to his job. He said he could not do that under the terms of the retirement package he had accepted. Furthermore, he said he had no interest in doing that or in working part-time. He thought about some volunteer work, but he rejected that as "more corporate babble." We continued in that vein, and he said he had not given volunteering much thought.

We talked about death and its permanence. We spent some time on that, and he also admitted that it was a rash try on his part without much forethought. Nevertheless, he felt he had spent the last two years feeling adrift and unprepared for the type of life he now lived. Our conversation continued around his family without him.

Discussion of depression, despondency, and fear took up much of our conversation. As we spoke, he began to realize that one thing he truly missed was the recognition he had received from his co-workers, his bosses, and his clients.

For many, both the subtle and significant perks of one's employment lie at the heart of life's fabric. Missing these rewards often eats at one's being once they are no longer a part of daily life.

"I thought that was just my being selfish, missing that," he said. "I didn't think I needed it so much. It is pretty frightening." He paused for a long time. "It is alarming to me, to think that I need people to clap for me so regularly."

We talked about reality and fantasy and how they often get mixed in one's life. We talked about how actors thrive on audiences and how people thrive on caring and respect and, while we often do not get the applause actors get, we receive handshakes, smiles, notes, and promotions that empower us to continue.

"I guess that is why I find every day so boring," Parker continued. "I am not getting my reactions, my prizes. You hit it on the nail with the word 'respect.'"

He slumped back in his chair. "I am a mess. I can't survive without the choir singing my praises. What am I going to do? What kind of a person am I?"

We could not end with those questions remaining undiscussed, so we spent time talking about many related areas.

As we ended, Parker said, "I almost blew it, didn't I? What a mess. I need to talk more with you. Can I sign up for a year of sessions?"

I smiled and replied that we would continue to meet. I suggested that Parker's work between sessions was to take care of himself, not take any wild actions, and think about some of the things we had talked about.

"Come back with questions," I suggested. "We have a pretty long lifetime ahead of things to consider that can provide the respect we all need."

I knew that Elena would be an effective and diligent watchdog, looking for any signs that indicated trouble during the time between sessions. Honesty is essential in therapy. Trust is also, but it takes time to be sure, and being sure is vital.

Over several months, Parker regularly came for his sessions. He had many questions, concerned that he was different from others in his feelings. Reassurance and medication helped him feel comfortable. He began to investigate volunteer opportunities and tried two, one of which he enjoyed. His natural ability helped him to assist the organization he selected become more successful. He became a mentor to two young people who wanted to move up in their jobs.

"You know," he said one day, "retirement can give people an opportunity to try things they never considered. It is not all travel and shopping and sitting at pools with cocktails.

There is a whole world out there that I knew existed but never really thought about in-depth."

"I have learned a lot. My wife and I are volunteering at the same place, and we are enjoying it together. It is a different life that I am living, and I am grateful to have it."

"And you know what?" he added. "We even have business cards. One of life's perks!"

Chapter 12:

The Tiger Tamer

Luis lived in a world that few people knew. It was a world of exotic cats. To be specific, Luis' life was one with tigers.

These were the wild beasts most people admired from a distance. Yet, Luis knew these cats and knew them well. The 500+ pounds of sinewy muscle wrapped in soft orange and dark-striped fur were his challenge and his companions. They stimulated him and gave him purpose. They were his universe.

Luis was "on" in the Center Ring. He managed five tigers alone, proudly exhibiting his control as the cats went through their paces. They jumped through rings of fire, stood on three feet, and stayed uncharacteristically still on their platforms.

Luis stood tall and gestured majestically, his movements a combination of orchestra conductor and skilled ballet dancer. The cats watched. Luis' body braced as he cracked his whip, commanding each tiger to speak in turn.

When the cats roared, Luis was in his element. He loved the roar of the tigers even more than the roar of the crowd. He had worked to learn extreme control. He never wavered, never flinched. He knew one false move could break his connection with the cats, bringing disaster. Luis kept to a strict routine, one he practiced at every moment. He walked it, talked it, lived it.

Luis showed his honed skill when one of the tigers menaced. Staring into the eyes of the wild beast, he would coax him back, back from the brink of rebelliousness, onto its place on the stand. One sensed the tension as Luis moved cautiously, controlling every movement of the defiant cat while ever aware of the other cats, watching.

Luis lived one pounce from death. He knew it.

He had never wanted an ordinary job. He had tried, but neither the people nor the work suited him. Living on the edge was exciting for him, always with the potential for danger. He relished the power of control, the ability to dominate the beasts.

Luis did not explain his life to anyone. His demeanor, his walk, his rigid carriage showed them. He was proud that his was a feat shared by few others.

His encounters with people were guarded, as if a tiger was always close. He didn't relate to ordinary things or people. In truth, nothing else in life mattered—not food, clothing, housing, or people. It was only Luis and his cats.

At night, his sleep was restless with the excited anticipation of the next day's danger. At times, when the tigers invaded his dream world, he would get up and move to Center Stage and perform, commanding the cats until he almost collapsed from lack of sleep. The cats were always in his head.

His obsession with the cats grew. He began to prepare for seven tigers in the ring, not just five. The time and energy spent in training began to exhaust him.

Soon the cats beckoned most nights. Their roar was distinct and taunting. Luis responded, but the stress took its toll, his mind teetering between control and collapse. Others noticed and tried to talk with him, but he pushed them away, knowing they could not understand.

Luis could feel his control in the ring waning. Sometimes the cats, all five of them, needed more commands than were safe to give. He faced them fearlessly as always, but one day he noticed an almost imperceptible quiver as he held the whip.

The cats sensed it instantly. And, in that exact second, Luis knew they knew.

He could see it in their eyes as they stared boldly back at him. He could see it in the way they responded, just a half-second delay before they followed his command. Testing. He could see the defiance. He knew he was losing control.

Luis said nothing, but others noticed. His walk slowed, and he spoke little. His eyes, rimmed in black, told of his nightly battles with worry about the cats. He wore out his shoes, pacing. He never passed a mirror without staring into his own eyes, practicing the look he used to control the cats. He held his whip and moved it slowly, watching his arm for any sign of tremor.

Luis continued to perform, but now he was content with five cats, no longer dreaming of seven. His anguished pacing and checking of his arm were relentless. He cut back to three cats, not daring to challenge the two younger ones in the ring.

His walk revealed what he could not accept. His carriage became stooped. He walked toward the center ring with a visible slowing of his gait and opened the cage door with a tinge of hesitancy. The cats watched with menacing eyes, their tails lowered in warning. Luis stared into their eyes, knowing they sensed the change. He knew they knew.

One day, bound to his bed by fear, Luis failed to rise. He could no longer face his beasts and the danger.

That day the hospital staff met. Luis was trapped in his struggle with his cats, unable to control them, unable to control the delusional world in which he lived.

The hospital staff decided. Luis must stay. With his mind locked in his inner world, his body must be locked up for his own protection.

"Luis must stay!"

Chapter 13:

A World Without Vision

Ben called my office and asked to come and speak with me. He said a music friend had recommended me since he understood I had been involved with the symphony world.

He knocked at my door and I opened it to find a tall, handsome man with a white cane, which he used to lead himself into my office.

Sitting in a chair, he began to tell me about his life and that he was blind due to a skiing accident. We talked at length about his accident, his rehabilitation, and how he functioned in his day-to-day life. Ben had taken advantage of many of the opportunities provided by organizations for the blind but said he was only able to function poorly in daily living activities. He then began to talk about his difficult adjustment to a sightless life.

"I am truly having a miserable time. I encounter almost hourly frustrations because I am sightless. I am so angry that I cannot drive and that I will never be able to drive again. I have not sold my car. I sometimes just sit in it and think about the times I drove without truly realizing what a gift it was for me. I have forever lost my sense of independence. I feel so incompetent all of the time."

"I have difficulty making sure my clothes are in order, and that I am not wearing clashing colors," he continued. "I have had to learn to feel the material that my things are made from, so I can at least guess what I am putting on in the morning. It takes so much time, and most of my shirts feel identical. Cooking is a nightmare, just like the horror I have traveling around the city. This is my city. I have lived here all my life. Now I have to ask people which way to turn to get to another street. I always get lost. It is just embarrassing."

He continued talking about all the difficulties he had as a sightless person. Then he spoke about his career.

"I was a violinist with a symphony orchestra and held that position for over twenty-three years. I love music, and I love my violin. However, after my accident, I could no longer remain part of the orchestra because of the requirements to read music for each performance. While I know much of the music repertoire that they play, I cannot read the adjustments the visiting conductors want."

He described the adjustments. These were the bowing notations on the violin score, written in for each performance by the concertmaster in conjunction with the visiting conductor. Bowing notations, inked in above the notes in the violin score, tell the direction of the bow, pressure, and such throughout the composition. They direct the violinists to move their bows in the same way. Since his symphony orchestra had many visiting conductors, these scores required reading of the accommodations for each performance. It was the same with the newer compositions he had not played before and that the symphony now contracted to play.

"At fifty-one, I am lost! My career is over, and I do not know how I can continue my life."

Ben had never married since he felt that music was his only needed companion. He had some family out West who had been very kind and helpful, but he felt he could not turn to them since they had families of their own. Some of his friends still kept in touch, but Ben said it was not enough to give him his life back. He said he had pretty much retreated into himself, only going out when he absolutely had to get something.

As we talked, I could feel the pain and despair of this talented musician, with significant health and life challenges which most of us, fortunately, do not have to face. Ben said he wanted to talk, and maybe, just maybe, I might have some thoughts about his life. It was a difficult challenge for him and me. His depression was evident, as were his feelings of helplessness.

We began by talking about music. It was evident that music was Ben's life.

"I live a life of massive frustration now," he said, "often enhanced by my significant anger, which explodes because I cannot see. Things take so much longer to do, and I often stop and leave some things that should be completed. Since I lost my vision, I have not used my computer, and I do not think I want to try any training with a visually impaired specialist since it would be much too frustrating. I have enough trouble trying to use my phone."

At my request, he brought his violin to some of our sessions, and I asked if he could play new music if he heard it. He was not sure but was willing to try. Like most skilled musicians, he had a trained ear and found he could play some new songs after listening to them. We talked about the possibility of teaching violin.

He sat back and thought about it for a while and said, "I think most students would not want a blind music instructor. I don't think I could do that."

It was evident that he would not find a position in a major symphony orchestra such as he had. I suggested a possible local orchestra with talented players and a permanent conductor for its concerts, but Ben was concerned about his inability to read new music. I had collected copies of several programs from their last three seasons, and it was all music he had played before and knew well. This orchestra did not have visiting conductors. It was possible that they just played the more traditional versions of classical music without the continuous changes.

Finally, after we talked about it for a while, Ben agreed to meet with the conductor of the local orchestra. He was pretty nervous about it, but afterwards Ben reported that the meeting had gone quite well. The conductor invited him to come to a rehearsal with the local orchestra. Ben went and, after the rehearsal, the conductor was very interested. In fact, he asked Ben to be a guest violinist for one of their concerts.

Ben was tentative about the opportunity but agreed to try. He reported that the rehearsals were a great success and he invited me to attend the concert. His solo performance was a delight.

Ben felt quite comfortable with his contribution to the orchestra that night and enjoyed the accolades from the audience and the orchestra members. His spirit was greatly improved by this return to his love of performance.

The conductor then asked Ben if he would consider being on their substitute violinist list. Although he was quite nervous about it, he agreed to go to some of their rehearsals to see if it would work.

He invited me to attend the first concert in which he was a substitute. Again, Ben was successful, and the possibility that this opportunity would continue was promising.

Back in my office, we again approached the idea of teaching violin. Since I had never played that instrument, I asked Ben if he would teach me how to begin, and he agreed. We tried, and he found it easy to show me the beginning steps and, thus, potentially show another student how to begin to play.

Connections with the local orchestra also produced an opportunity for teaching violin to young students. Some of the musicians did this in their spare time. The auditorium where they played was in a local high school, and it had music rooms for teaching. Ben agreed to teach one of the students who had just applied for lessons. A violinist from the orchestra agreed to work with Ben and the student for the first few lessons to see how things went. Ben was pleased with the class and the possibility of continuing as a teacher.

Despite Ben's initial concerns about his continued possibilities as a professional musician, we discussed these new opportunities that enabled him to be involved in music again. He began to realize that he could continue to play and that teaching was enjoyable. He found that the students were curious about his blindness but were not negative about it. They actually found it interesting and respected Ben for his ability to play without seeing. He soon had several budding violinists as his students. He also had several opportunities during the orchestra season to substitute for violinists, and was invited to be a soloist several times.

Ben was pleased to have these new opportunities. Some of the orchestra members had a small group that played at local events and private parties. They often got together just to play music, and Ben enjoyed these occasions and his new friends. He became comfortable with their offers to drive him to these events.

After about a year, Ben said he was no longer lost. The daily life of being blind continued to be difficult and undoubtedly would always be so. We discussed getting a guide dog, and he agreed to consider that option.

Following his unexpected blindness, Ben's life had some positive turns. He discovered fulfilling opportunities and new friends to enjoy. Bouts of depression still appeared occasionally, but not as intense or as often as before. He frequently dropped into my office to tell me that he felt more confident given that he has a legitimate place in the world and could continue with the music he loved.

Ben was courageously—and successfully—moving ahead in his newly challenged world.

Chapter 14:

Choices

On Tuesday, a disheveled, bent-over man was brought to my office by Kate, a social worker who worked at a nearby clinic.

"I told Rico he needed to see you," she said as they walked into my office and sat in the chairs near the window. Rico sat uncomfortably and kept his head down, looking at the floor.

"This is Rico," Kate said.

I held out my hand and said, "Hello, Rico." Rico did not move.

"He speaks some English," Kate said, "but with difficulty. Just barely enough to get by."

Both Kate and I switched our conversation to Spanish. When I asked Rico some questions, he looked up and shook his head. His face was sad, wrinkled, and seemed covered with dirt. I assumed correctly, as I later discovered that he had been living on the street.

Kate asked Rico if she could tell me about him, and assured him that it was safe and essential to do that. Rico nodded.

Over the following time, I learned that Rico had come to New York from Puerto Rico about a year earlier with his wife and young son. He had gotten a job cleaning offices but, due to a series of circumstances not of his doing, he lost that job within weeks. As a result, he had no money for food and stole groceries from a nearby market. His wife did not know that.

He also met a drug dealer and decided he could make some money selling drugs. Kate said Rico told her he never took drugs himself but was arrested the first time he tried to sell them because the "buyer" was an undercover police person.

He was put in jail and released a week or two later with a required return court date. He said he was ashamed and afraid to tell his wife, but when he went back to his apartment his wife and son were no longer there.

He told Kate he looked everywhere for them but could not find them. He could not get into the apartment, either, so he slept on the street, under a bridge near a subway station, where he went when it rained. Every day he looked for his wife but could not find her. He was beaten by other street people and moved his location, but kept looking for his wife each day. He had no money, no other clothes, and no real food.

One day a police officer stopped him and found out he had missed his court date, so Rico was put back in jail. Again he was released to the street, but the next day he passed out and was brought to an emergency room for treatment.

As Kate spoke, Rico watched me carefully. I listened and asked him if the story was true as it was told, and he nodded, "Yes."

The Emergency Room social worked had called the clinic where Kate worked. It was, a facility for indigent people who needed mental health help. Kate brought Rico there after meeting him at the hospital. When he came to my office, he had only been out of the ER one day, and had spent the night in one of the clinic beds while Kate tried to find a place for him to live.

In my office, Kate told Rico she would have to go back to the clinic to work on some things for him. She told him to stay in my office and talk with me, and she would return to get him. He agreed.

Rico spoke a little after Kate left, a combination of English and Spanish, and I learned that his name was not Rico. That is what they had called him at work because he came from the Island of Puerto Rico. He said his wife thought it was cute, so he kept the name. His real name was Pablo.

I asked him why he slept on the street rather than go to a shelter. He answered that shelters were dangerous, and he felt safer on the street. He spoke haltingly, but poured out his soul to me. He was fearful that his wife and son were gone or hurt. He missed them, but was so ashamed of what he had done. He insisted again that he never did drugs and that was confirmed by the testing done at the clinic. He was afraid his wife would not understand.

He told me he had worked as an office cleaner in Puerto Rico and made just enough money to rent a tiny apartment and buy food. He said he walked five miles each way to work six days a week on the Island.

Rico said he came to New York City because he thought he could have a better life for his family, but it had not worked out. Now his family was gone and he lived on the street.

His story was atypical of many of the people who sought shelter on the street in New York City. Rather than suffering from mental illness, which caused so many to become street people, a string of difficult circumstances had put him there.

At this point, he was afraid and anxious. He expressed a sense of complete hopelessness. He was in a strange city with no one to turn to and a missing family and no way to take care of them if he found them. He did not know what was going to happen, but asked if there was any way we could help him find his family. I explained what Kate would do to look for them. We could not promise anything, but we would try. He bent his head and put his hands together in prayer.

"I so wish to find them," he said. "I love them so much. I will do anything to find them and work hard."

Rico feared the police and going to jail, but knew he had another court date. I told him about an attorney we often used who would help him. It was the first time I saw a spark of hope in his eyes.

We talked for a long while that afternoon, and when Kate returned she told Rico that she had gotten a studio apartment for him in one of the Center's apartment buildings. She also talked about some of the ways she was working to get him interim financial help.

We planned that Rico would come back to my office in two days and continue to talk. I told them that, the next time we met, I would ask the attorney to be here to review papers related to his case. Rico said, "Gracias" so many times, I thought he would lose his voice.

So, Rico became my patient. The attorney helped get his drug sale dropped with the condition that he continue with therapy, to which Rico had already agreed.

Session after session, I learned more about this young man. He presented as a kind and caring person and, once he had a place to live safely, he looked his age of 27 rather than the 50 years plus he had appeared in our first meeting.

Months as a street person took their toll physically as well as mentally. He was fearful, anxious, and depressed. He also constantly said that he did not deserve a place to live because he was not working for it. Rebuilding his sense of self was painstaking and taxing. He was so ashamed of what he had done. He worried about his family and was afraid that his wife would not accept him even if his family were found.

Finally, I felt Rico was strong enough in many ways to take on a part-time job in maintenance in the building in which he lived. He was pleased to have a purpose.

All the while, Kate diligently searched for his wife and son. It took months, but she located his son, Emilio, through the school system when he entered pre-K. Through that contact, she met Rico's wife, Mara.

Mara could not believe that Kate knew where Rico was and that he was alive. She was so afraid he was dead.

She said, "I thought he might have been beaten up and killed. But, you know, you just feel something, and I felt he was not dead, but how would I ever find him in this city. I knew he loved me, and he would not go off with someone else. I knew he had to be lost for some reason. Emilio and I had to move, and I thought Rico would never find us."

Mara told Kate that she looked for Rico on the street but never saw him, and she was afraid to report it to the police. She and Emilio now lived in a basement studio, and she worked part-time cleaning apartments so that she could be home all the time with her son when he wan't in pre-school. Mara cried and cried when she heard the news.

Kate called me, and when I told Rico that we had found Mara and Emilio, he sobbed. He paced the office and said, "Oh God, will she believe me? Will she forgive me? I left them!"

Hours later, Mara and Emilio came to my office. The reunion was so tender and tear-filled for all of us. Indeed, the sun does shine extra brightly on some days.

The difficulties of life in the big city for two young people and their son did continue. However, the family's dedication to each other and determination to do well made their reunion successful. Rico's ability to believe in himself again definitely helped.

This story does end well. Sadly, though, it is a story not often replicated on the streets of major cities in our country. If only it could be.

Chapter 15:

Therapy and Friendship

Sometimes therapy involves talking; sometimes it involves doing.

The call came on a Friday.

"Can you come to see me?" She asked. "I want to sit with you and talk. I need your help. I hope it is not too much to ask of you."

Madame Auchincloss was a noted concert pianist. She was a well-respected and sought-after teacher of piano performance at some of the most prestigious music schools across Europe and the United States. Deciding to retire to her childhood home, she had returned to Paris full-time after dividing her time for many years between France and New York City. She felt that her life would be more comfortable in Paris, speaking her native language.

Our relationship had morphed over the years from my being her piano student to her being my patient. She had come to see me several times about professional issues that she felt were affecting her life in an unwanted way. Ten years before, she had told me she had Parkinson's disease. We had spoken at great length at that time. She returned to therapy again when her husband became gravely ill. Now she said that a level of rigidity had set in due to her Parkinson's. The disease was progressing in an expected yet unwelcome manner.

I agreed to visit Madame Auchincloss immediately. She was my piano teacher, my patient, and my friend.

For me, the next few days were busy making contact with physical and occupational therapists to learn more about approaches used by these professionals as Parkinson's progressed. Armed with as much information as I could absorb in a few days, I flew to Paris.

My mind raced as my taxi arrived at her home. I rang the doorbell with a sense of trepidation. Henri, her houseboy of many years, opened the door and smiled as he gestured for me to enter. The afternoon light from the window cast a gentle glow on her face as I stood in the doorway to her music room.

"Bonjour, Madame Auchincloss," I said softly.

She lifted her head slightly and held out her hand. "Ah, you are here. I am so glad you arrived safely. It is so good to see you again."

She gestured for me to sit across from her.

I had not known what to expect. It had been several months since I had seen her. As we spoke, I could see that her once straight back was now bent forward, and she struggled to keep her head up to maintain eye contact. It was apparent that the disease was progressing.

After we ate and covered subjects familiar from years of friendship, she spoke quietly about her medical condition.

"It has been difficult," she began. "Until a few months ago, I was doing well. Now, I cannot play all the music I used to play. I do not always have the strength or agility anymore. I am limited to those compositions not requiring extreme octaves, as my body is robbing me of flexibility. This disease has not taken my music yet, although it may. I am not sure what I will do then. My music—my music is my life."

She spoke about her days of depression, not being able to play the music she loved. She told about endless tears without having all her music to interrupt and bring pleasure. She was worried about what lay ahead for her.

"My doctors have been honest," she continued, "but, I am not thrilled with the therapy I have had. Maybe there is nothing more they can do. I feel there has to be more. I must find more that will help."

As she spoke, I heard the determination of this world-renowned concert pianist. She had reached the heights of her profession through tenacity and dedication, fighting to overcome the odds she faced for many years. Now, it was a battle for her life as well as her life with her music.

We spoke late into the evening. I told her that I had brought some ideas from therapists in the States to see if they might help. I suggested that perhaps we could share them with her doctors and therapists over the next week. She was pleased and cautiously optimistic, and said she would make those arrangements.

"Before we retire, let us play," she said.

With Henri supporting her, she walked to the piano. He had replaced her bench with a chair and, as she sat, Henri wrapped two shawls around her frail body and fastened them to the chair-back to keep her upright. She placed her hands on the keyboard of her grand piano and nodded to me to sit at the other grand facing her, as we had for so many years.

"I will begin," she said. "You will recognize it. You will remember where to join me."

I listened as the music of Mozart's *Piano Concerto 21, The Andante*, filled the room. I smiled that she chose that piece. It had been my first major concert piece. She began to play, and I was lost in the beauty of the sounds, almost missing the part where she indicated I should start.

Before I arrived in Paris, I had been concerned that she could no longer play or would not want to play. Fortunately, her bent body had absorbed the ravages of the disease, and her hands had been spared so far.

We played Mozart. Her performance was rich and authentic, expressing the composer's intent; she, a consummate musician.

As we played, my mind drifted back to afternoons in her New York City apartment, sitting at the dual pianos, recreating our interpretations of the music. I was always striving to meet her exacting requirements. I heard her precision, her clarity in each note and chord. I heard Mozart speak through her playing.

At the end, she sat, silent. I did not speak, not wishing to break the mood of the moment.

"You need to practice more," she admonished. "Natural talent needs practice and tweaking, but you still play remarkably well."

My heart sang. Violet Auchincloss was never profuse with praise.

That evening, as night fell, I thought back across the years to the stern face of my music teacher. Demanding and somewhat austere, she was devoted to music and her pupils. She was idolized. She traveled between New York and Paris, and I was lucky that my family also traveled between the two cities so that I could continue my piano study with her. Lessons were several times a week, and I both loved them and dreaded them, afraid I would not meet her expectations. It was always a delicate balance, juggling the demands of the music world with the outside pursuits of childhood and teen life.

She gave me the gift of music that enriched my life. I needed to find the words and a way to help her at this time in her life.

The following days were filled with visits from her doctors and therapists. They all came to her home and shared their work with us. They listened to what I had learned from my therapist contacts in the States. They made plans to develop exercises that would help reduce the rigidity and keep a level of flexibility that would enable her to continue playing the piano. Henri stayed for each session, learning how he could help her with these new approaches.

True to her fortitude, she was intensely involved in the planning, going through each of the devised exercises. Each afternoon she was exhausted but ready to continue. Her determination was fierce.

In the evenings, after dinner, we played the piano and reminisced. We talked about the gifts she gave to people, what she had done to make music a part of so many lives. We spoke about the physical difficulties of aging and disease. We talked about how some people can hear the music of the ages in their heads. Our words covered many worlds.

She was concerned about her end of life. Her husband Marcel, an accomplished cellist, had serious illnesses for the final years of his life. He was always in pain and mostly bedridden. Violet Auchincloss was his primary caretaker. She feared being ill, as he had been, and she had done much reading about Parkinson's and death. She asked if it was true that most people died with Parkinson's rather than from it. We spoke about statistics and causes of death. She had already well-researched the subject.

Her husband had decided, after years of illness, he wanted death with dignity. He and his wife had traveled to Basel, Switzerland, where it was possible to have legally assisted suicide. After staying there for a week, he had entered a well-known clinic that provided assisted death. I had spoken with him—and with her—hours before he died. I visited her the following week when she returned to Paris.

Madame Auchincloss spoke softly about that time.

"Marcel knew it was time. He often said he probably should have planned it earlier, but it was evident that it was time then, and it was an extremely sad but correct choice. I want you to know that I believe that I have several years of life left in me, and I want to be as physically and mentally able as I can. I will work to strengthen myself, so I can continue my music. You have given me the way and the will to continue. But, I have made the decision. When I feel I can no longer live the life I want to live, I will go to Basel. I will not ask you to go with me. It would be against your professional oath. I hope you understand my choice. I will not talk about it further."

On the last day of my visit, she asked if I would play with her so that we could tape some of her favorite pieces. We did.

She began to play the Rachmaninoff *Piano Concerto #2*. I played and knew when she would wait for me to play alone, filling in the expansive octaves. I worried I would make a mistake. I had not played this composition in years. The music and the aura of the sounds seemed to take me to another world, a world in which only music filled my life.

As we finished, Madame Auchincloss broke the silence. "You do not play as much as you should," she said. "You have a gift. Technical ability, yes, but even more important, you feel the music. I hear the composer speak as you play."

I was elated. I had played only for myself for a while, certainly for no one as insightful a critic as Violet Auchincloss.

Slowly, I found the words, "It was you who taught me to not only learn the music but to know the life of the composer, to feel his happiness and his pain. It has made a difference not only in my playing but in my life. It has helped me to understand people better."

That evening, we played again. She gave me the music and began to play an aria, a magnificent arrangement of *Nessun Dorma* from Puccini's opera, *Turandot*. As we began, I was captured by the music and the story. It was as if we drifted back over the years and reclaimed the times of special joy we shared then and shared now.

As we said goodby the following day, Madame Auchincloss said softly, "Your visit, your words, your help, have enabled me to feel strong again. You have made it possible for me to continue."

"Remember *Nessun Dorma*," she continued. "The aria is translated as, 'None shall sleep,' because of the difficult task ahead for Calaf. But Calaf replies, '*Vincero*—I will win.'"

Madame Auchincloss smiled. "Your visit has enabled me to say, 'I will win.' *Merci, mon cher ami. Merci.*"

Acknowledgments

Special thanks go to many people.

To Ryan Jenkins, my long time editor at Peterboro Press for his belief in this book;

To Suzie E. for her friendship and suggestions that kept me on target despite significant life-altering hurdles along the way;

To the members of my writing group for their continuous support;

To Bill, who is always there for me;

To Dr. Richard F. who gave me the gift of time to write this book;

And to my patients who have shared their lives with me.

This book is written because of my remarkable and resourceful, "Renaissance Man," Roy.

Roy's excellence as an insight-oriented psychiatrist provided endless opportunities for me to learn. His

exceptional support and optimism never ended throughout his life. He encouraged me to help others understand
psychotherapy by writing these stories. He has truly been
my North Star.

About the Author

Dr. Doonan studied Classical Rhetorical Criticism in college which qualified her to be a Greek Empress but the job market was quite slim. So, she took her knowledge of Plato and Aristotle and their writings on how people think, and earned advanced degrees in Psychology and Psychiatry.

She has spent her career working in clinical settings and in her private practice in New York. She worked at a Rehabilitation Hospital in New York; served as a consultant to The College Board in New York City; as a consultant to the staff and students at the Medical School in Guadalajara, Mexico and to the Brockmann Foundation, in Guadalajara, Mexico. She has served on the Boards of National and International Foundations, was the Founding Director of a nationally replicated program for College Students with Learning Differences.

Dr. Doonan is a recognized authority on brain functioning and a requested speaker at national and international conferences.

She is a classical pianist, and a writer, has served on the Boards of several symphonies, and in her spare time, showed her champion Maltese Dogs.

A working mother who balanced career and family, she reports she still remains "somewhat sane."

Made in the USA
Middletown, DE
12 January 2022

58508245R00115